Dearly Departed

Dearly Departed

Everything you want to know about the afterlife

GEORGINA WALKER

inspired
LIVING

ALLEN&UNWIN

First published in 2008

Copyright © Georgina Walker 2008

Inspired Living, an imprint of Allen & Unwin
83 Alexander Street
Crows Nest NSW 2065
Australia
Phone: (61 2) 8425 0100
Fax: (61 2) 9906 2218
Email: info@allenandunwin.com
Web: www.allenandunwin.com

National Library of Australia
Cataloguing-in-Publication entry:

Walker, Georgina.
  Dearly departed : everything you want to know about
  the afterlife

  ISBN 978 1 74175 0010 (pbk.)

  Psychic ability. Spiritualism. Future life.

133.9

Set in 11.25/15 pt New Caledonia by Bookhouse, Sydney
Printed in Australia by McPherson's Printing Group

10 9 8 7 6 5 4 3

To my mother, Agnes Gibson, for without her spiritual gifts, wisdom, guidance and love I would not be the daughter, mother, grandmother and psychic I am today. With love and gratitude I thank you.

Names have been changed all but for a handful

Contents

Appreciation

I am truly blessed with the support and encouragement of so many people along my spiritual path. For without such love and belief in my work, this book would not have been possible.

Especially:

My friends Kerrie English and Louise Mills—telephone confidants, morale boosters and loyal dear friends who have shown undying devotion and support over the many years of our friendships. Alison Yeung and her friend Mr Mo; Cecilia Canning and Jasmine Raj—thank you for opening doors and opportunities to experience new cultures, fulfil dreams and just have some fun! To 'The Royal Family' who gave me back my confidence—you all remain special within my heart and soul.

My media family—Kyle Sandilands and Jackie O who had the courage to be 'different' in radio formats, challenge the norm and bring the gifts of psychic predictions to the airwaves—a huge thank you. Derek Bargwanna (DB), the man with the Midas touch in radio production who just knew we would click and work well together—thank you your friendship, skill development and mentoring and for those crazy times away on the media circuit which will always put a smile on my face—love your work! Maggie Hamilton of Allen & Unwin whose intuition and dedication bring the world of spirituality to the world of books—thank you for belief in my work, your wisdom and your encouragement. Lauren Finger and Karen Williams—much gratitude for your sensitivity, guidance and knowing ways. Sabina Collins for her magic work in editing my manuscript, warm chuckle and twinkling eyes—couldn't have done this without you.

My wonderful clients and ALL my friends—thank you for energies exchanged.

Testimonials

Losing my brother to a drug overdose was very sudden and extremely hard to deal with. The feeling is just indescribable, and words can never do it justice. The reality of never hearing him talk, laugh or seeing him develop into the man he deserves to be is heartbreaking. Losing a brother is like losing part of yourself. Because he left us so suddenly, I was desperately holding on to anything that slightly brought back a memory of him. I had so many questions, but above all just wanted confirmation that he was okay. I made my booking to see Georgina and was counting down the days to be reunited with him.

One of the first things Georgina mentioned was that Jimmy had an addictive personality. This threw me a little, as I'd not said anything about the way he died. She was able to pick up a few other character traits, which made me convinced that she had chanelled Jimmy. During the reading, Georgina also mentioned a dispute around music. I laughed instantly as I knew what that meant—Jimmy and I were always at each other's throats about what music we wanted to listen to. A couple of days before my reading, my mother and I were listening to some music and reminiscing about the countless times Jimmy would sit in the lounge room and turn up his music so loud that I had to run downstairs to tell him to turn it down. Georgina confirmed that Jimmy was present when we had that conversation.

Georgina mentioned a lot of things that were accurate, and throughout the reading I really felt Jimmy's presence. I felt as though I was able to have a conversation with him again, and for a moment it felt like he never left. I still think of him constantly, and I'm extremely afraid to let go of his memory. Although it's nothing compared to having him back, Georgina gave me an opportunity to find closure and to say things I was unable to say to him before he died. She gave me a priceless gift and I can never thank her enough.

Cathy Le, Panania, NSW, Australia

My father-in-law recently passed away, and Georgina immediately picked up that he wanted us to know he was definitely around, and would send us feathers. I came home straight after the reading and bang—there was a gorgeous white feather on the floor in our bedroom. There was no explanation for it being there. I called my husband, and he said he was looking at a feather inside a closed room and couldn't figure out how it got there. You could have knocked both of us over with a feather! It's nice to know he's around.

Nicola Mills, Rozelle, NSW, Australia

My mother died when I was seventeen. We had a difficult relationship, and I always wondered what she'd think of me as an adult. My reading with Georgina left me without a doubt that Mum has been with me every day since she passed. The information Georgina passed on from her included a nickname for my son (Ducky), who was born after she died, and an acknowledgement of my dislike of Mum's curried sausages! It was mind-blowing. Georgina accurately described how my mother died, and gave many details that could only have come from her. I feel as though I've heard all the things she'd have told me if she were still here, and I now feel resolved and happy to let go. Thank you, Georgina, for sharing your wonderful gift.

Jodi Dickson, Chipping Norton, NSW, Australia

Georgina's accuracy with regard to details about my departed mother was both hair-raising and extremely comforting, knowing she's at peace and still with us in spirit.

Rocco Polito, Cromer, NSW, Australia

Georgina did a reading for me on her 'Supernatural' radio show. All I said was my father's name three times. No other information was given. From this, Georgina told me how Dad passed away, his favourite foods and what I meant to him, and she even told me about things my father has seen me do that no-one knew about. For example, I'm putting together a DVD to play at his one-year ceremony. I found an old video of him dancing—I'd never seen my father dance. That was only a few nights before the reading.

I called my partner and said, 'Quick, you gotta see this!' I couldn't believe Dad was dancing. In the reading, Dad said to Georgina, 'I danced before and I will dance with you again.' He was watching me put the DVD together.

The information Georgina gave me and my family was 100 per cent accurate. Georgina gave us solid reassurance that there is an afterlife and that Dad was okay. The pain will never go away; however, knowing Georgina had spoken to Dad helped us deal with it so much better. I can't thank her enough for the reading. She has a gift and she uses it to help people like me, not only to deal with grief but to reassure us that there is an afterlife and we're not alone. Although I can't see Dad, I know he's still around—if it wasn't for Georgina I'd still have my doubts. After the reading, there's no doubt at all. I would recommend Georgina to anyone. Her accuracy is absolutely incredible.

Nadia Dable, Dural, NSW, Australia

I was a barrister with 34 years in active practice when I first met you in July 2005. For some five years prior to that, my mind was disturbed and consistently centred on discovering the killer of someone near and dear to me. Your very special gift at my first meeting with you, and that too within half an hour, resolved all my doubts and ever since then my life has returned to being more meaningful.

Guna, Kuala Lumpur, Malaysia

I made a Dearly Departed appointment with Georgina Walker and on arriving for my visit, I handed her some items of my son's as requested. She asked me three brief questions: What was his name, what was his nickname and how long ago did he die? She then closed her eyes and for the next fifteen minutes proceeded to talk about Steven. I was laughing, crying and just shaking my head as she got him so very right. She did not have my expressions or responses to inspire her as she had her eyes closed for the whole time. She is amazing and accurate and I am very glad that I went to her.

Kathy McDonald, Avalon, NSW, Australia

I had a Dearly Departed reading with Georgina where I connected with my father. I lost my father at eleven and I'm now 27. I was prepared for Georgina to say things I could relate to; however, I was not expecting such incredible detail and precision. Georgina relayed messages from my father that were very touching and true. I felt I received closure from him and could relate to his messages as an adult rather than a child who lost their dad. This was a fulfilling experience that I will keep with me for life. I'm blessed to have interacted with Georgina who has such an amazing talent that others can benefit from.

One message I received from my father through Georgina was a song, 'Edelweiss' from *The Sound of Music*. This song was sung over and over in my home when I was a child, and when we travelled to Austria before my father's passing, he arranged for edelweiss to be picked from the top of the Alps and we still have the pressed flowers today. This was a very touching message for me, and when I went home that evening I found a music box my dad had bought for me that I'd forgotten about, and on the top of the box was the word 'edelweiss'. I played the music box and it still worked after eighteen years. My dad definitely connected with me. I was blessed to have experienced this with my dad. Thank you, Georgina!

Eleisha Martyn, Northern Beaches, Sydney, Australia

A very short note to thank you for today's reading—I hope to visit you again when you return from your trip as I found great comfort in your ability to translate my father's messages. It was really lovely to meet you and I wish you well on coming ventures. Have a wonderful holiday.

Cristina, Five Dock, NSW, Australia

I had a Dearly Departed reading with Georgina to contact my mother. I learnt several things about my mother that I did not know—like she was a big fan of Lucille Ball and she liked *Mother & Son*. I had no idea—it was only after I asked others in the family that this was confirmed. There were also family rituals that I could not remember because I was the youngest child. These were cooking pikelets as a special treat; and each child having their own eggcups to stop fighting. It was an exciting experience and I would recommend it to anyone with an open mind.

Larry, Marrickville, NSW, Australia

Introduction

There's a reason you've been drawn to this book. You may have lost someone very special—a family member, close friend or pet. Or perhaps you're caring for someone who is asking you difficult questions such as these:

'What's it like when you die?'

'Is there really life after death? What's it like? Is it heaven or hell?'

'Will we see each other again?'

'Is there such a thing as communication from the other side?'

'Can they forgive me for not being there when they took their final breath?'

'Have they enough clothes to wear?'

'Did they link up with Dad?'

'Has he passed over safely? How will I know?'

'Why have they left me all alone?'

'I can't go on like this—the pain's too much. What can I do?'

You may relate to some of these questions, or perhaps you're soul-searching; looking within at your own mortality or your own purpose; testing religion, philosophy and science—pushing the boundaries as to your own unique reason for being. You may be bargaining with God: if you're a better person now, will you reserve a seat in heaven rather than hell? Why do we suffer so much in this lifetime, and what's the point?

Messages from beyond can be delivered when you least expect it—sometimes by a distant stranger holding a bear with the date 2004 on it! Our 'dearly departeds' do communicate with us from the other side, giving solace, understanding and hope to continue on our life's journey. Sometimes their messages are so subtle they can come to us through a song, a movie, words spoken in a conversation with a friend, dreams or thoughts that just pop into our heads. Spirit will find a way when there seems no way. I'm not a scientist, researcher, theologian or scholar. I'm a psychic medium who on a daily basis works with the living to tap into the other side—the afterlife.

Come with me on this journey, be open-minded and allow Spirit to speak to you through these stories and give you hope, encouragement and a sense of comfort that there's something more than in the breath we take—there's another world beyond this one!

1

Message from beyond

Death is not extinguishing the light; it is putting out the
lamp because the dawn has come.

Rabindranath Tagore

Tired from a frantic year's workload, I was keen to board the
plane to start my overseas vacation to paradise. I had chosen
Samoa, where there would be no mobile phones, just quiet
sandy beaches and gentle ocean waves—seven days of sheer bliss.
There was still some time for last-minute duty-free shopping before
my flight was called, and I always treat myself to a new bottle of
perfume with each overseas break. It's as though the holiday destination becomes branded in a sensory experience. Then, each time
I put on a particular scent, I am instantaneously transported back
to the scene and the memories of times spent in different lands
come flooding back.

It seemed silly at the time, but on this occasion I was drawn
to a sign that said 'Teddy bear with every purchase'. Now I didn't
actually need a teddy bear, especially one that I'd have to carry

out of the country and then bring back a week later stuffed in my suitcase with my other holiday purchases. But the feeling was overwhelming—I needed to buy that perfume. Was it the name 'Giorgio', which was similar to my own name? Well, the fragrance smelt rather yummy, but I really wanted the teddy bear. It beckoned me from the large sign over the perfume counter. I had a feeling I had to give the bear to my son Brendan's new girlfriend, Latoya, and to tell her it was from her sister Claira.

When the assistant was packing up my purchase, I asked where my bear was.

'There aren't any left—they've all gone,' she said.

'Are you sure? I really feel there's a bear in the shop I have to have.'

She rolled her eyes. Off she trotted to the storeroom, while I waited.

'You're in luck, this is the last one,' she said. It was a bear, the size of a large dinner plate—fat, happy, wearing a yellow and white striped jumper, with a large red 'G' embroidered in the centre. Attached to one of its paws was a large satin label that read 'Giorgio Beverly Hills 2004 Collections Bear'—strange, as it was March 2006, but that was the bear that went with the package deal.

Surely Latoya would also think it odd to be given an outdated bear as a gift. In fact, I didn't know too much about Latoya, as I'd only met her briefly when she and Brendan were passing through Sydney on their way to the outback for the haymaking season. Brendan had mentioned to me on the phone that his new girl-friend was from a large family, and that one of her sisters, Claira, had died in a car accident.

Brendan's 21st birthday party was a month later so I packed the teddy bear in my bag, along with other surprises I'd bought the family while I was away, and boarded the plane for the short one-hour flight. Like all young people, they were keen to open their presents from overseas. I pulled the bear out of my suitcase and handed it to Latoya, saying: 'This is for you, from Claira. It's a gift from her to you. I feel she wants you to know she's thinking of you.'

Latoya looked at Brendan, and tears welled up in her eyes as I relayed the story of the bear and gave her a whiff of the perfume.

Georgina, this is just like the sweet-smelling perfume Claira liked to wear, and 2004 is the year she died. She was fourteen when she died. She was staying with our dad in another state. We were very close growing up; there was only three years difference in our ages. Mum and I had only spoken to her over the phone just before Christmas and were very excited to hear her say she would soon be coming home to live with the family again.

I remember Mum gave Claira a warning that day about getting into cars with drivers who were unfamiliar, reckless or who'd been drinking. I was to learn later the significance of her message—you see, Mum had a secret she hadn't shared with me or anyone else in the family. I too had a secret—it was so weird—about three days before Claira died I was watching television. It was a random thought, like I was daydreaming. I saw my uncle getting a telephone call saying

Claira had died. I just knew it would be on the road, in a bus or car.

Christmas came and went. Late Christmas night, I was snuggled up in my bed reading, when suddenly the light flashed on my mobile phone—there was no ringing sound, just the flashing of the light. 'Claira,' I thought. I'll always remember the time on my phone—11.15 p.m. The next morning was Boxing Day and the downstairs phone rang. Perhaps it was the thought of Claira the night before, plus the weird experience I had had when watching television, that made me rush as fast as I could to answer the phone. No-one ever rang me on this phone, preferring to contact me on my mobile. So the thought of wanting to answer the house phone was out of character.

As I stood at the top of the stairs, it was too late; my uncle had beaten me to it. I saw his face and he started to shake, and I just knew it was about Claira and that she had died. It was my worse fear, the unusual vision I had experienced several days before had become a living reality. I was so scared—I knew what he was going to tell me. I was dreading the news. Claira had been killed in a car accident late the night before.

Mum needed to be told. My uncle and I lived out of town near the beaches in those days, so we drove the one-hour car trip to Mum's place. I cried non-stop the whole way—but I knew I needed to be strong for my mum. As we approached her home, I tried to pull myself together. But Mum acted as

4

though she already knew. When she saw me, she said, 'Please don't tell me anything bad.' She started to run around the house like a crazy woman.

You see, Georgina, the secret Mum hadn't shared with me was that she had a dream, a premonition, prior to speaking to Claira on the phone that day, where she'd seen a car rolling over and over and someone thrown through the front windscreen. We learnt from the police that my father's girlfriend was drunk that night, and she was behind the wheel of the car as it sped out of control, rolled and Claira was thrown out through the front windscreen. Apparently she was sitting in the back of the car, sandwiched between her boyfriend and another passenger—wearing no seatbelt.

We were told she died instantly. However, we were to learn later this was not the case. You see the policeman's wife had come out to the accident site that night and heard Claira's boyfriend calling out, 'Libby, Libby—where is Libby?' Although we called my sister Claira, in fact that was her middle name. Her first name was Elizabeth, and Libby was the name some people chose to call her. Her boyfriend's cries prompted the policeman's wife to go searching with a torch in the surrounding roadside and scrub, and thankfully this was how she discovered Claira who was badly injured.

We were so grateful she did this, otherwise Claira may never have been found. The woman stayed with Claira until she passed away. The accident and circumstances weighed heavily on her mind, and she felt we should know the true facts. One thing she mentioned was that just before Claira died she was smiling. Yet the coroner's report said she had eight fatal injuries—so how could she possibly be smiling? It was one of the things about the accident that I felt puzzled about— I had no explanation as to why someone in such bad circumstances would ever consider smiling.

After the funeral and church service, we were driving to the cemetery when Mum told me of her dream and the premonition she had. I can recall that day so clearly—it was raining, and as they lowered Claira's coffin into the ground, the rainwater was trickling down the sides of the coffin. People had scattered rose petals on top of the coffin and as I looked inside her grave, I felt so helpless. I just wanted to jump into the plot and be there with Claira—I didn't want her to be alone. I was devastated, and I truly believed I could never ever recover from her death. So I made a promise to Claira that when I had my first daughter she would be named Claira, after her.

The healing begins

Just over a year later I holidayed again with Brendan and Latoya. Latoya's mother, Mary, was keen to meet up with me once more, as we had met briefly before. This time she wanted me to experience some of her traditional Island cooking. Mary is proud of her strong indigenous roots, hailing from the Torres Strait Islands, off the far north coast of Australia, scattered as far away as Papua

New Guinea. Their food is wonderful—cooked slowly in banana leaves, with loads of coconut milk, vegetables and meat. I was to experience a true feast of the Island kind that went from evening, to breakfast then lunch—a smorgasbord of delights.

It was during our times together that I was able to discuss Claira's passing with Mary. On our previous meeting Mary was too emotional to talk about her daughter's death; however, this time she was more open. I was blessed to be able to share stories of my clients who have had Dearly Departed readings, and relate the experiences and lessons I had learnt as a psychic medium from the messages imparted to the living from those who had crossed over as they gave proof that life indeed lives on in another dimension, and how at times they have left messages and symbols to their loved ones that they are indeed thinking of them.

It was later in the week that Latoya shared with me the comfort she personally felt when listening to these stories. One particular theme that played over and over in her mind was hearing the case stories of the loved ones who, in their final hour, would speak to someone standing by their bed or close to them. They would call their name, have a conversation with someone as though it were a two-way street, listen and respond, yet family and friends standing by couldn't see anyone else present. Some did recognise the name being addressed, but these people had already crossed over, leaving those present feeling their loved one may be hallucinating.

But now Latoya understood that these were returned loved ones who manifested as the dying person's guardian angel or spirit helper, here to pave the way for the transition of the spirit to the other side, making the forthcoming journey of the soul easier with someone familiar, comforting and loving.

'Georgina, now I know why Claira was smiling before she died. I believe it was our Aunty Robyn who came to collect her. She died in 2000, and she and Claira were always close. Claira would always give her a big hug and smile when they visited. It makes me feel good and peaceful to know that when Claira died she was not alone.'

Mary shared her dream with me, and we talked about the 2004 teddy bear experience at the airport. Latoya giggled and asked, 'Had you noticed the colour of the bear, Georgina?' Well, actually, I hadn't taken any particular notice. I presumed it was gold. Rushing upstairs to retrieve the bear, she plonked it on the coffee table right in front of me, along with a beautiful photo of Claira. I couldn't help but smile—the 2004 teddy bear was not gold, as I had presumed, but a gorgeous shade of chocolate brown. I knew exactly what Latoya was thinking.

'Can you see the family resemblance? We're not-fair skinned at all—more like the shade of the teddy bear!' The significance of the purchase, the message and now the colour of the teddy bear were even more significant than I had thought. Mary explained to me that in her culture and society 'signs' are very much entrenched in their way of life. She saw the significance of the teddy bear, date and message—even down to the letter 'G' (as GG is my pet nickname in the media)—as signs that Claira had manifested to show those closest to her that even from the other side, she still honoured her cultural roots and identity.

Message from beyond

As I put the finishing touches on Claira's story, I have some wonderful news to share—I am to be a grandmother again later this year! Latoya and Brendan are expecting their first child, and, yes, it is to be a girl, already named Claira!

2

A cry for help

For this is he that was spoken of by the prophet
Esaias, saying, the voice of one crying in the
wilderness, prepare ye the way of the Lord, make
his paths straight.
The Bible, Matthew, Chapter 3, Verse 3

The Language of Spirit has no boundaries—we all have the ability to communicate across time and space. Your mind can travel to any place in this world and beyond. When you pray, meditate, daydream and ask for help, you send a vibration into the universal energy field seeking an answer, solution or healing. As this is emitted, it is also received!

World War II times were uncertain, which prompted the spiritual 22-year-old British naval officer Roy Gibson to buy a gold cross in Colombo, Sri Lanka, while his ship was in port. He had the letter 'R' and his fiancée's initial 'A' engraved on the piece, one on either side of the outstretched arms depicted on the cross. For him, this would symbolically protect the wartime sweethearts until they could be together.

For 20-year-old Agnes, her only link to Roy was the cross she wore around her neck and his letters, many of which arrived in pieces as the censor's scissors cut out highly sensitive location and event information. There were no privacy laws in those days, and Big Brother had the final say. Should those innocent, chatty letters from one sweetheart to another fall into enemy hands, perhaps they would alert them to potential spy activities or locations of ships and troops on the move that could give them the upper hand and turn the war to their advantage. Many of the letters Agnes opened resembled small strips of ribbon rather than pages of a letter. But a letter was a letter, no matter how small. Even just a few words meant he was alive.

In England on Easter Saturday 1945, at 7.30 a.m., Agnes arrived for work at the factory where she was employed as a seamstress to sew war uniforms for the troops. The factories in wartime worked seven days a week, even on public holidays, to push through the large quotas of clothing needed by the soldiers. Agnes was combing her hair in the ladies' restroom when the mirror took on the appearance of shimmering water and waves and all seemed dark. She heard Roy's voice cry out—'Agnes'. She felt great fear and backed away from the mirror. As her back touched the wall, she fainted and slid down to the floor.

That evening she wrote to Roy, telling him of her experience. Several days later, a workmate told Agnes she'd been to the local movie house, and on the world news screened before the movie was an announcement that the *HMS Indefatigable*, where Roy was an engine room artificer, had been hit by a plane and seventeen men were dead.

As the plane hit the deck and burst into flames, the order was issued to seal the engine rooms to keep the ship afloat. Roy knew his fate and called out, 'God save me' and 'Agnes'. Thousands of miles away, the voice of Roy in the dark engine room was 'heard' by his fiancée and the emotions 'felt'. Spirit had delivered his words.

The ship's steel deck, rather than a traditional wood one, saved the men as the flames were extinguished quickly. The orders to seal the engine rooms were never carried out.

Roy wrote to Agnes that night. Very little was left of his letter due to censorship, but one sentence had been left complete. It read, 'Yes, it certainly was April Fool's Day', indicating to her that something had happened that day that he could not discuss openly.

Some things are inexplicable, such as a voice heard audibly from one person to another with no wires or vehicle to send information. Yet for this couple, proof of the existence of unseen powers and forces would ultimately see them take a spiritual journey and quest that covered a lifetime together.

They married in 1946 upon Roy's return to England, and a few years later migrated to Australia and had one child—you guessed it—me!

3

I heard his voice

If you cannot observe it, then you must meditate,
contemplate and imagine it, it is wondrous that if
you contemplate long enough, then
eventually you will see it.
When you are able to see something that cannot
really be seen—then it is wondrous.
Henry Chang, *Dragonfly* Magazine, Volume 4

'Green, green is the valley where I lie.' The words came rushing through my ears. It was a man's voice. I knew I hadn't imagined it. It was real. I instantly recalled how the kids at school would say, 'If you hear voices in your head, it's a sign of madness.' Was I really mad?

I hoped the other people sitting in the circle heard his voice too. Would they believe a ten-year-old? Then suddenly, before my eyes, I saw an elephant trample a garden bed. It was crystal clear, right down to the texture of its skin and the colour of the flowers.

Surely they'd have seen that, I thought.

It seemed like an eternity that we all sat in darkness. I was the only child in a roomful of ageing adults who had come to investigate the supernatural, wanting to develop their psychic gifts or have proof of the existence of a spirit world.

We'd been instructed to sit in a large circle and concentrate on a vase of flowers that a redheaded, well-dressed woman had placed in the middle of the room. Perhaps we would see, hear or feel something. A message, a prediction or some form of proof of another sense—a sixth sense.

We regularly made the one-hour drive from my parents' home in the leafy northern beaches into the bright evening lights of a fast-moving Saturday night in the city of Sydney. We'd park the car and make our way to the theatre district, where I was allowed to select a small bag of handmade chocolates. The treat, I realise now, was a bribe to keep me silent for the night's activities.

Walking up the old stairwell, it seemed as though the creaky stairs were singing their own mantra: 'Come—be prepared, come—be prepared.'

You couldn't help but notice the assortment of people in the large room. Some were well-manicured in appearance, others seemed out of place. They were lost souls looking for an evening out—perhaps some light entertainment or a sudden rush of adrenaline with a ghostly encounter.

The old iron chairs were already in neat rows facing the front of the hall, where a small table covered with a lace tablecloth had been placed. On one side of the table were, neatly placed, the Bible, a collection bowl for donations and a jug of water with two mismatched glasses. There was a chair on either side of the table—one for the guest medium or psychic and the other for the convener.

My bag of dolls and toys become increasingly more boring as the weeks went by, and the chairs were most uncomfortable as I wiggled and squirmed. Sometimes I listened with intent to the guest speaker, questioning whether it really was Red Eagle or Cleopatra who the medium had brought through—their hand gestures and unusual voices all sounded fake to me. Other mediums seemed to shine as they talked, and I sensed a genuine interest and belief in what they were saying.

I clearly remember the night my parents went forward for a healing to give up their addiction to cigarettes. They threw their packets away there and then, and neither of them looked at a cigarette again. This was a place where miracles and healings occurred. But as a child, boredom was setting in and the novelty of chocolate had worn off. So what had I to lose that evening when the call came to make ready for the development circle. That night I would participate—give it a go.

Chairs were arranged in a large oval shape. My parents sat opposite me. I was sandwiched between two strangers. The convener placed a large arrangement of flowers in the centre of the circle. We were told that we needed to concentrate on the flowers—by doing this we may be able to tap into the spirit realm and receive messages and information from the other side for those participating in the development circle. Then the lights were switched off, and a veil of silence fell. I sat very still, a little nervous, a little scared, but something exciting was stirring within my soul. I waited for a sign, something that would show me what it was like to be a psychic, or bearer of spiritual messages.

The silence was endless. I wished time would just speed up so I could have the supper that followed. In the 1960s, only rich people could afford chocolate biscuits and the supper table was guaranteed to have a plate or two.

Then it happened. The voice, the message, the vision. I heard quite clearly, 'Green, green is the valley where I lie', then I saw a large grey wrinkled elephant trample a colourful-looking garden. That was it—two very different 'signs' which didn't make any sense, but that's what I experienced. As the lights were switched back on and my eyes adjusted, I witnessed eager adults discussing with their neighbours what they had experienced. Then the convener, who had also been sitting in the circle, rose from her chair and walked to the centre of the circle, right next to the flower arrangement.

'Can I have your attention please?' she asked. The chattering stopped, and all eyes became transfixed on the convener. 'I would like everyone present to share their experiences with the group— anything, just anything, no matter how small, simple or even if you feel it is unrelated. Speak the truth, I am encouraging you to develop. Perhaps you had impressions in your thoughts or feelings. Some may have heard a message, observed a vision or sensed something within their bodies.'

I came to realise later that her disciplinarian manner was in fact there to help, support and develop our confidence, gifts and potentials. If we didn't learn to share what we experienced, then the path of development could be impinged. But as a ten-year-old child sitting in a room full of adults, I found this form of confrontational questioning very intimidating and scary.

'I will come to you first, sir. What did you experience?' The man slightly blushed as words rapidly fell from his mouth. 'Now the lady next to you—madam, tonight what occurred for you?' It was obvious as she made her clockwise move around the circle that no-one was going to escape the 'dreaded questioning'. Finally she came to me—it was now my turn. I was quietly confident. I had a stillness within me that I had never experienced before, an inner confidence that I was not indeed mad—it was real. I plucked up the courage and told the group exactly what I had experienced.

I could hear giggles, whispers and grunts, as though they were thinking, 'This child's in fantasy land'. Inside I felt an anger that was not natural. My face coloured, I was embarrassed. I'd made a fool out of myself. I was a failure at my first attempt.

Thank God supper was served and I had something to occupy myself with. I was starting to learn that food was a comfort in trying times. I noticed two adults from the group approach my parents. One was the redheaded lady who had placed the flowers in the circle, and the other was a man. There were whispers and occasional glances my way.

The lady had come to tell my parents about the prophetic message I'd delivered—the only one in the roomful of adults, from a child. It was from her deceased husband, a pilot whose plane had crashed. He was buried in a green valley in Wales. The flowers were to commemorate his death. The gentleman recounted that during the week a visiting circus had come to his suburb and an elephant, the star attraction, had escaped, made its way down the street and eventually trampled his garden, destroying it. Through the feedback from these two people, my parents came to realise the common thread or vibration was around flowers. They had come to the weekly circle to develop their potential, but in fact it was me who showed great potential as a psychic and medium. My path was set. My apprenticeship to the spirit world had begun.

4

The secret

The secrets of this earth are not for all men to see, but
only those who will seek them.

Ayn Rand

The weekly development sessions held at my parents' home
were spin-offs from their investigations on Saturday nights
in the city. There were about four couples who lived close
by and shared a common interest in wanting to explore the world
of the supernatural. Once a week they would visit my parents' home
and assemble in the lounge room.

My bedroom adjoined the lounge room, and at times I would
sneak out and peer through the door to try and catch a glimpse
of what was happening. I can remember a woman sitting in a chair
with my mother standing behind her—Mum had placed her hands
on the woman's head and was saying prayers. Years later I was to
learn that my mother was a healer and what I had witnessed was
a healing underway.

The Saturday trips to the development circle stopped abruptly after I gave my first public demonstration of my gift—when I accurately gave the message to the woman whose husband was buried in Wales and when I saw the elephant trample the garden. The reality was that if my parents continued to be seekers and develop their own potential in the psychic realms, I too would develop rapidly; and in their wisdom they felt it best that my gifts develop along a natural course rather than be spurred along through weekly intense training. After all, I should have a 'normal' childhood and experience life suitable for my age. They believed that if there was to be a divine use of my gift, life would unfold in divine timing, not their timing.

So I was thrust back into church life, where there would be religious discipline, training and a belief that was structured and would lay a firm foundation for any work in the spiritual realm that may be called upon later in my life.

We had no extended family in Australia—our family consisted of Mum, Dad and me. Once in a while the small, square, laminated dining table would be extended to allow two more chairs and places for anticipated guests, perhaps a friend of mine, or neighbours Mum and Dad had invited over.

My parents met at the local village dance. Much of their courtship and early married years revolved around activities associated with church life; something they were to adopt when they moved to Australia. Familiarity was comforting, yet we had a secret. Behind closed doors, all manner of religious philosophies and non-traditional healing practices were discussed. From their informal studies and practices I had received a dramatic absentee healing in the 1950s for my rheumatic fever by the famous English healer, Harry Edwards. It was the subsequent healing that alerted my parents of my gift.

I recall waking up one night, sensing something very strange. I sat up, to see multicoloured lights zooming directly at me, like power surges. I was frightened. They danced around me, behind me and into me. I wanted to call out to my parents, but I froze. The only way to get to my parents' bedroom at the other end of the house was through the coloured lights, so I thought it safer to stay where I was. Eventually I must have fallen asleep.

The next morning, rapidly recounting what had occurred to my parents, the discussion became more like an interrogation. They wanted to know everything that had happened, realising I'd experienced a psychic phenomenon.

Several weeks later they received a letter from Harry Edwards, who, at the time, was considered England's most renowned spiritual healer. The contents of the letter detailed the healing he did for me—and the date. And yes, it was the day I saw the lights—they were the healing lights of Spirit. Through the power of intention, powerful prayer and kind thoughts, healers like Harry channel divine energy directly to the person who needs healing. This very same power is available to you right now. Start by monitoring your thought processes as you think of people you know—are your thoughts pure, kind, warm and caring? In time you will learn to edit negativity as you project only positive thoughts towards those in need. Keeping a gratitude diary or a prayer list may allow you to concentrate on individual's needs and grateful accomplishments. You were born with the most powerful computer—your brain. Allow it to work miracles not only in your life but in those of others.

Mum read tea leaves for her friends and practised laying on of hands on folk who visited our home. She had made a vow to God that she would never charge for her gifts, and consequently we had a linen cupboard full of scented talcum powders and boxes of lace handkerchiefs, given as a form of appreciation. I silently vowed to myself I would never do what my mother did.

Her mother had told her to keep her gift a secret. She had given her first healing to someone at the age of six, had prophetic dreams and had amazing experiences with astral travel, where her astral body was able to separate from her physical body, resulting in flying dreams. This allowed her to visit foreign countries and witness events as they unfolded, the accuracy of the information she had gleaned while she slept confirmed several days later through friends or family. Her mother was fearful that if she told people, they wouldn't understand and she'd be considered 'different'. My parents wanted a fairly normal life for me, so I had to promise not to discuss our family secret.

I remember one day a painful spur in my father's foot instantly disappeared as Mum prayed for a miracle. She felt comfortable doing her healing and prayers in her bedroom. The walls were pink and are still pink to this day. Heavy lace curtains tried to conceal the Venetian blinds that tried to obscure streams of Australian sunlight that penetrated during the day. The highly polished floor-boards had pink scatter rugs. The double bed had a pink and cream satin bedspread. It was here they both sat that night as she held Dad's aching foot in her hands and asked silently for God's divine intervention and healing. In front of their very eyes, the swelling and pain disappeared. Some would say this was miraculous, but for my family it was considered natural. 'Ask and ye shall receive' was one of the quotes they loved to use from the Bible, their source of comfort and rules to live by.

My mother had always told me: 'If ever you need me, all you have to do is call out my name and I will hear you and find you.' To me, it was as natural as the other parental golden rule: 'Never go with strangers.'

I hadn't needed to test the 'power of the spoken word'; I knew from my parents' training that I was divinely looked after, and if ever I felt I was in danger or in need of some form of help or assistance all I had to do was ask! Yes, ask aloud or silently the divine power and all would be well.

One day, upon returning from Sunday school, I realised I hadn't taken my house key. My parents had travelled that day to clear a block of land they owned that was covered in lantana, a noxious weed that the local council was keen to see eradicated. Facing a day sitting on the front veranda was not a welcome option. The words sprung into my head: 'All you have to do is call my name . . .'

For the second time in my life I would participate. I had been successful in getting a response at the Saturday development circle, so I thought I had nothing to lose by trying it out one more time. There I sat on the white cane chair, part of a setting that to this day sits in exactly the same spot. I called out in my mind, over and over, 'Mum—come home, Mum—come home.'

My parents had just unloaded all their work tools from the car when my mother turned to my father and said, 'Gina is calling us, we must go home'. He wasn't happy. But there's one thing my father had learnt from the events of the war, and that was to listen to my mother's inner voice. They hurriedly packed up and came home.

I recall as the car came down the driveway Mum calling out, 'What's wrong? What's the matter?'

My response was simply, 'It works.' I can assure you by the look on their faces they were not amused with my matter-of-fact answer. But that Sunday I learnt a powerful lesson—telepathy exists.

5

Power play

I was shown a fledgling learning to fly. Its first efforts
were very feeble. But as it used its wings more and
more, they became stronger until it found the freedom
of flight and was able to soar to great heights and fly
great distances without any effort. I heard the words:
Faith comes with practise. Live by faith until it
becomes rock-like, unshakable, and find the
true freedom of the spirit.

Eileen Caddy

My teenage years were taken up with weekend basketball,
ballroom dancing, my ear stuck to the transistor radio
listening to my favourite heart-throbs—Elvis Presley and
The Rolling Stones—and, more importantly, boys. I had no inclination to be involved in anything mystic. I fell in love with the
boy next door—well, around the corner—and we married just
before my nineteenth birthday. He was 22.

Our first child, Rebecca, followed five years later, with the rapid onset of my gift returning. As I lay on the delivery bed, suddenly I felt myself leave my body as though I was floating up to the ceiling. I looked down, and I could see myself in labour with my grandmother holding my hand. But she'd died when I was a young child. The only time I spent with her was when my mother and I made the six-week boat trip back to England when I was three. My nan's health was in rapid decline—she had never met her Australian-born grandchild and my mother knew that trip would be the last time she would ever see her own mother. We spent six weeks at Nan's house in the Midlands, a region known for its wonderful pottery ware.

Three years later, our second child, Andrew, was born. But after nine months their father walked out the door. The affair had started when Andrew was three months old. Now I was forced into single parenthood. Rebecca had been an easy child, but Andrew had asthma from ten weeks of age. He was very unsettled, had great difficulty with his breathing, and he was in constant need of attention to administer medication and therapy.

Did I know or sense anything? I was too involved in raising my children to listen to the small voice in my head. Busyness is like deafness to the spiritual world. When you're quiet, you're more able to tap into their energies, observe, learn, listen and act upon the whispers of advice they send. Words from a song may strike a chord within your heart; a conversation with a friend may reveal the advice you've been praying for; the book or magazine that stands out from the rest on a shelf may hold the answer to your needs.

I was searching for answers—angry at God that what had seemed perfect had come to an end. How would I manage? What would I do? I was 27 years old with two small children.

Within two years I had met and married a farmer and moved to live in outback New South Wales on a sheep and wheat station. I was to spend fourteen years in the wilderness of drought, hardship, economic devastation and emotional abuse. The bonus was the rapid development of my spiritual gifts. My dreams were vivid and prophetic and I acted upon them with gusto—but that's for another book.

During this time I had a spiritual visitation from the deceased statesman Sir Winston Churchill. He told me, 'One day you will walk the paths of kings and queens, for this is what you are to do.' He recounted what was to unfold in my life in the forthcoming years. There was no way a poor farmer's wife could ever meet with a king or queen.

My third child, Brendan, arrived after a very difficult and trying pregnancy. By the time he was three, I had packed up the children and headed for the nearest city, some 130 kilometres away. For the first fortnight I fed them potatoes, chips, potato cakes, more chips and pancakes. They didn't mind one bit, which was lucky as that's all we could afford until my first pay cheque came in from my new job as a casual TAFE teacher.

Trying to juggle single parenthood once again, I had five part-time jobs. But having gained a reputation for insight and prophetic prayer, I found that people were knocking at my door at all hours asking for help. It was at this time, when finances were so low, that a friend asked me, 'Why don't you charge for your gift?' The words of my mother that she would never, ever charge for her gift bounced in my ears. It had been engraved into my psyche. The wise friend advised: 'Then charge for your time or ask for a donation. Your children need to be fed, and you need to live. After all, singers, doctors and actors get paid for their talents, why not a psychic?'

Life started to resemble some form of normality when I had a dream that changed my life. I woke suddenly to hear a voice telling me: 'You can't love anyone else until you love yourself. Give yourself a present.' Boy, did I want to know what that present was. I fell back to sleep and was visited by a beautiful Asian woman who I now know to be one of my guides. She showed me a journey that I was to take—I would visit the Land of the Swords where there was much work for me to do.

I moved back to Sydney to work in the field of health. I wanted a 'regular' job where no-one knew that I had supernatural gifts. We all have a blueprint of the soul, and if there's to be a lesson or you're off-course, Spirit will pull the rug from under you to point you in the direction of your soul's purpose. There's a saying I have always recalled—'for much is given, much is sought in return'. Spirit had once again provided another detour, another lesson in my soul's evolution, but the price was indeed sacrificial.

One day a staff member was crying and I confided that I could help. But she wasn't to tell anyone what I could do. I asked her to allow me to take a piece of her jewellery home so I could do a reading for her. This is called 'psychometry', one method a psychic can use to 'read' energies or vibrations stored in jewellery, photos or clothing belonging to a person. The following day I gave her ring back along with a tape of the session, again asking her to keep it a secret.

Within days, someone else turned up at my desk wanting a 'reading'—the word had spread. It would be through this person's association that I would later become the Royal Psychic.

Wisdom and insight is one thing, but to see corruption through your abilities can be life-changing. In my managerial position, I was faced with the harsh reality of blowing the whistle on the director of the program. My staff and friends turned their backs, and I went on sick leave. I tried to return several times, but no-one would speak to me or even acknowledge I was there. It took eighteen months to prove my allegations were correct. The director lost his position and a number of staff roles changed. I think I'm the only psychic who has been sent to psychiatrists by the government and told I was sane!

The royal psychic

I was 45 years old and ony had one dollar in small coins to my name when a telephone call changed my life. It was a man, saying, 'I can't find my daughter, can you help? Interpol can't locate her and you have been recommended to me.' The posh, English-sounding man's voice echoed in my ear. If there is one thing I have learnt working in this field is regardless of who we are or where we live, we still tend to ask the same questions about life and death at some time in our lives.

Immediately I sensed his daughter had eloped and gave him information of her whereabouts. He then requested a more detailed reading and would courier photos of the young woman with the condition I must courier the reading back to him ASAP. Only having one dollar in my purse, I asked him to cover the costs. When I enquired who I was speaking to, all I could remember was the name Mohammed. Later that afternoon I was to learn from our mutual contact that he was a sultan and his father was a ruling king.

Excitedly I rang my mother to fill her in on the day's happenings. 'Why would a sultan ring my daughter?' she said. 'Georgina, you've been under enormous stress. You don't think you've imagined this?' I was devastated that my own mother couldn't comprehend or believe what I was saying. But when the courier delivered the parcel and I tore it apart, there was the royal seal. I drove to my mother's home, pushing the envelope and the contents into her hands saying, 'Now do you believe me?'

I received several more phone calls from the sultan before his consort rang me. 'Georgina, it is now time that you hear my voice' were the words that echoed down the phone line. We chatted for some time and she told me how my predictions had given her great comfort. 'We would like you to come and holiday with us,' she said. 'At the moment we're very busy with royal duties, but in time we will have you come over and stay.'

One morning I awoke with a premonition that I would soon be travelling to their country. I pulled out my suitcase from under my bed, gave it a good scrub, dried it on the back veranda and waited. With the two eldest children now independent, working and living away from home and my youngest living on the land with his father I found myself in a unique position—totally free to be led where Spirit directed me. I just knew I was going there—the small voice in my head was telling me to be prepared. The very next day, in the wee hours of the morning, the phone call came: 'Pack your bags—we're taking you on holidays to the summer palace.'

I left with $150 in my pocket, $50 of my own and $100 my mother had given me. It was a leap of faith that I left with so little to stay with people I'd never met—in another country, of another faith. The initial nine days would eventually extend to a 30-day stay!

The plane was late arriving and I was concerned as a driver was being sent to collect me. In fact, the sultan and his consort had sent their own personal chauffeur, who took my bags from my hand and escorted me to a huge gold Mercedes parked right in front of the international terminus—not in the parking area, but right in front—wow!

Several days later when I became familiar with the driver, I asked why people waved and stared at the car. He explained that the car numberplates, with two gold swords and a crown, signified this was the car the sultan or his consort travelled in.

As we drove to the palace, I had a small giggle to myself. No-one was going to believe me when I get back to Sydney. Pinch yourself, Georgina. My heart was pounding as we approached two large black wrought iron gates bearing the official royal crest in gold. A policeman came forward from a little standalone booth to peer into my side of the car, then he nodded to another policeman, who hit the controls for the official gates to open, allowing the vehicle to move forward into the royal grounds.

The car slowly came to a halt, right in front of a door at the extreme end of the palace. I was to discover later that this was the family's private entrance, used during the night or on unofficial occasions. I had anticipated a maid would open the door, but in fact, the sultan did!

'Georgina, you have arrived! Come, come in, rest, and have a drink,' he said. He was dressed in a very casual colourful silk skirt and slippers that made a shuffling noise as he walked on the highly polished marble floor. His consort, who was stunningly attractive, had dark brown flowing hair to her shoulders and was wearing a very vivid coloured kaftan.

It was a moment in time that was now set—friendships formed that would last a lifetime and, regardless of who we are, the universe speaks to us through signs, through others. To this day, the consort and I email each other nearly every week. We are two women from opposing ranks in society with a common bond—the love of children and family.

Over the following days I holidayed in five palaces in their capital, coastal and regional centres. It was at the main palace while standing on the large royal ceremonial balcony that I asked the sultan: 'What are those javelin-like devices with flags attached face-down in the lawn?'

He turned to me and said, 'Why, don't you know, we're known as the Land of the Swords. They're the nine ceremonial swords for the celebrations tomorrow.'

I thought of the visitation of the Asian guide in my dreams six years earlier and what she had told me—that I would be going to the Land of the Swords as there was much work for me to do. The prophecy had become reality.

Later that evening I shared the vision with the consort. The next morning, as per usual, the sultan and I had breakfast together. 'Georgina, my wife tells me you have a very special story to tell me about the Land of the Swords. Can you please tell me the significance? This all sounds so fascinating.' So I rambled on, telling him the whole story, the predictions and to date what had happened.

'So you are saying it was indicated or prophecised, as you call it, that you would be coming to the Land of the Swords. But how can that be? Are you saying that it would appear there is some plan or knowledge that knows what lies ahead?'

'Yes, I call it the "Blueprint of the Soul"—it is our birthright,' I replied. 'Through premonitions, dreams, prophecies and spirit guides and angels we can be privileged to see glimmers of this path to come. Talking about spirits, did you know that you too have spirits in this palace? I saw two last night in my bedroom wing.'

The colour drained from the sultan's face, and he put down his coffee cup and looked me straight in the eye. 'What are you saying?'

I could see now that perhaps I was treading on ground that could be conceived as controversial. So I back-pedalled, saying how

I was excited to be given such a huge wing to sleep in. Then I realised that although his look was rather tense and he wasn't satisfied with my cover-up, he wanted to know about the spirits, so I told him.

'Well, I was just getting settled in bed when two spirit children started jumping up and down on my bed. Then they played the game hide-and-go-seek, and were once more jumping on my bed. They seemed so happy—I must have fallen asleep some time later.'

'Oh dear, Georgina, I ask that you not tell our children of your experience in that room. You see, that's the room we put the children in when they come to the palace.'

'Ah, now I understand, the spirit children were anticipating guests that night as the maid prepared my room. They would have been excited and looking forward to having playmates that evening. You know, some people say their children have invisible playmates— they chatter away to unseen children while they play with their toys, even calling them names. Parents feel their children have vivid imaginations, when in fact it is not of their imagination, they see further than most.'

I have to say the look on the sultan's face was not that impressed, more alarmed at learning that he had ghosts or spirits in his family's palace.

I looked forward to our morning breakfasts together, where we would read the local and international newspapers and have discussions—informal exchanges concerning the unusual world of the supernatural and spiritual kind. One morning, the sultan told me he had a dream the night before, in colour. He said he never dreamt, but since I'd come to stay and live in their palace, he'd started to have vivid dreams. He dreamt that his missing daughter would ring him and say she was coming home. And that she did. That very morning, the telephone call they had long awaited was received. Tears of joy we all shared. How different from the structural existence the outside world observed of this family.

My return date to Sydney had been changed several times to accommodate special events and receptions the royals were to attend and I had been especially invited to, but I had only packed two evening outfits, not realising that every night was a 'formal' event for this family. The sultan's father, the ruling king, had a very special event planned—The Banquet of Rulers—and an invitation had been extended for me to attend. However, the king had requested that I wear a dress. Hmm, I hadn't packed any dresses.

A dear friend of the royal family was commissioned to take me shopping for fabric. I chose a most magnificent French fabric—of course I later found out it was the most expensive in the shop—then rushed to a dressmaker, who had to work very long hours to complete the long formal dress and jacket. My arms had to be covered, as it was a strict Muslim dress code for the grand palace function. I was also taken to the royal hairdressers for a posh hairdo.

It was to be a very official and glamorous event. The sultan and his consort wore traditional attire—I have never seen emeralds as large as those around her neck—they were stunning. Totally gobsmacked, I asked, 'Are they real?'

In her more than gracious manner, probably silently wondering where on earth they'd found me, she replied: 'Yes, Georgina, they are not copies.'

It was such a regal and important event in the country's calendar, I needed my own escort. I had seen this man often around the palace and knew he was a personal bodyguard assigned to the regent. As we drove up the official driveway to the main palace, he placed his palm upright in front of me, indicating he wanted his palm read.

'I don't read palms,' I explained.

'Well, what do you do? I know you are here to make predictions.'

'I read handwriting,' I said, hoping this would silence his request. Then, to my total surprise, he handed me a menu with a sample of his handwriting scribbled across the top of it.

'Please read my future,' he said.

I told him I was off duty, here to enjoy a holiday not to work predicting individuals futures, but he insisted.

What could I do? I had to agree.

'You will not tell anyone what you have told me?' he said.

'No, of course not,' I said. 'This information is between you and me.' What did strike me was that his handwriting had the most amazing leadership abilities, and I silently thought his talents were wasted as a bodyguard and escort for me that night.

It was an exciting event. What a privilege it was to be invited, they even had me sitting next to two charming princes.

As was the custom for each special night out with the royal family, once back at the palace the consort and I had a cappuccino and excitedly talked about the evening's events.

'Did you find your escort helpful tonight, Georgina?' asked the sultan, smiling.

'You know, your bodyguard has far more potential than you realise. I think he's wasted in his position.'

The sultan, who was leaning on his consort's chair, nearly fell over. 'Please don't tell me you gave him a reading Georgina—you did, didn't you?'

I explained what had happened, and I sensed I was in big trouble and had really done something to break palace rules. I had assured the escort of his privacy and now I was openly discussing his desire for a consultation. But then a huge smile appeared on his face when I got to the part where I had said I was off duty.

'You actually told him you were off duty?'

'Yes.'

'I love it! You know, Georgina, he is the Deputy Police Commissioner.'

I must have lost the colour in my face, but the royals were in fits of laughter. Later the sultan told me, 'You're like a breath of fresh air.'

There was one more special event to occur, the eve before I flew back home to Sydney, and that was the sultan's official birthday party. I wore the same outfit I had worn to the Banquet of Rulers—again it was to be a very formal event. All guests were asked to be seated at their tables waiting for the arrival of the royals and VIPs.

Suddenly the music started playing, and we all had to stand to attention as the dignitaries walked in. The king, queen, sultan and consort were to sit at the large round table in the centre of the room, along with other royals who had flown in for the event. Once they were seated, a ring of security personnel surrounded the table, looking more like waiters than bodyguards. Silence fell on the room, and out of the corner of my eye I could see a woman walking towards the table I was seated at. It was the queen's lady in waiting. She came up to me, bowed and handed me a long rectangular box covered in the royal wrapping paper. It was yellow, with the crest of the royal family, and a handwritten thank you card. All eyes were now upon the exchange of gift and words.

'This is a gift from Her Royal Highness,' she said. She then turned and went towards the royal table.

I had been told that it was inappropriate to open presents until you were in the privacy of your own home, but I couldn't wait that long. I carefully undid the paper, exposing a beautiful gold and silver watch with the royal crest on the face and the queen's name. I did so want to thank the royal couple, and luckily I was sitting next to one of their advisers, so later during the evening he sought permission to take me to their table.

As we approached, I bowed, then touched the king on the shoulder (yes, another big mistake) and said, 'Okay, which one of us is psychic? I was going to buy a watch at the airport tomorrow!'

He grinned and replied, 'Psychic lady, you are too funny.' Even today, each time I return to his country for a visit and our paths cross, he never calls me by my name, always 'psychic lady'.

As I left their palace, the consort and I held each other and cried. Two women understanding that no matter what circumstances our birth paths take, ultimately we had one thing in common—we were both mothers who loved our children unconditionally.

My dream had been fulfilled—I had now been given the title 'Royal Psychic' by the ruling king—and it was time to return back to the dramas awaiting me in Sydney.

Fighting for what I belived was true

I came home refreshed and with renewed energy to continue with my legal battle over the corruption allegations. The human resources department of where I had worked called one of their regular meetings. It was always the same—would you consider resigning and we'll give you a reference and you can go and find work elsewhere? But I'd been advised that if I did I'd only be paid up until the time I left, and nothing after that. I didn't want to resign; I wanted to fight for what I believed was true.

I dreaded these meetings and the unsaid pressures and tension that I'd feel coming from those present. This particular meeting consisted of the human resources manager, a manager from another department, two other staff members and me. The HR manager made a comment: 'You're looking so much better than I've seen you look for a long time—has something happened?'

'I've just returned from an overseas holiday with a ruling king and queen.' Well, the body language said it all. Everyone at the table seemed to move backward, as if to say, 'Oh, dear, she really is mad, gone over the edge, delusional'. Then I proceeded to tell them that I had ample photos to prove where I had been. 'No,' I said, 'I will not be resigning—I'll be fighting this to the end.'

Ultimately, 'the end' saw me winning an out-of-court settlement and the ability to resume my position in management. I declined the offer to return. I had lost faith in the system and the organisational structure. Why would I want to return to an environment that was so hostile?

There was enough in my payout to rent an apartment, which the sultan found for me and was my referee, and to buy basic furnishings and pay outstanding debts I had accrued while off work for such a long period of time. At last I could fulfil a dream of assisting people with my gift as a professional psychic.

I returned to the Land of the Swords as an official guest at the 'formal wedding' of the princess. Yes, she had eloped to the country and place I had predicted. The dress code was strict for a Muslim wedding—long sleeves, long dress. I had put a lay-by on a beautiful burgundy outfit, but money was still tight as my court case hadn't been heard at that stage and my lay-by was overdue by two weeks and about to be put back into stock. I was very stressed, but Mum came to the rescue.

One Saturday morning, she rang to say she had prayed to my deceased father and told him of my situation. She knew within her spirit that she would win the major prize, $500, at bingo at the local RSL club. Would I come? She'd split the prize money with me and I could take out my lay-by. Yes, she did win. The following week she rang and made the same offer—that if she won first prize

I could buy shoes and a handbag to match the outfit. Yes, she won again. My outfit was literally 'heavenly decreed'.

I met people at the wedding who would become lifelong friends, and made connections that opened doors for me internationally, with clients and business opportunities in every continent of the world.

6

Welcome to the world of media

Words have the power to both destroy and heal. When words are both true and kind, they can change our soul.

Buddha

When I returned to Australia after visiting the royal family, my story was featured in national women's magazine *New Idea*, and I was then offered my own weekly psychic column.

Questions touch and affect not only the readers' lives, but also those of their families. Many write on behalf of a daughter, son, sister or friend, all seeking a little ray of hope and encouragement to continue on their life's journey. Others are looking for solace and messages from their departed loved ones—the grief almost jumps off the page as I read the words: 'I never had the opportunity to say goodbye. Can he ever forgive me for giving permission for the life support to be switched off? There was no choice, the doctors said he would be a vegetable.' Or 'If there was a God, why did he allow my baby to fall into the pool and drown? Prove to me there's a God.' And, 'I just can't go on living this life—why did she have to kill herself? She had everything going for her. Why didn't she come to me with her problems? Maybe, just maybe, I could have made them go away.' And more unanswered questions: 'I didn't make it to the hospital in time; she was gone before I arrived. Did she know I was trying but was held up in the traffic?'

Sometimes, I feel overwhelmed with this responsibility. How I would love to answer each and every letter and email that comes before me, but I humanly can't.

I ask that I be directed to letters that not only aid the writer, but others who will also read or hear and find among the words an answer to their burning questions. Some cover such thought-provoking questions as looking for their soul mate, coping with suffering and grief of a dearly departed, and there are those who ponder on or seek confirmation of the afterlife, begging for signs as proof that their loved one is now pain-free. 'Did they link up with family members on the other side? Are they now my spirit guide, or who is my spirit guide or guardian angel?' It's great when I receive confirmation of this very fact—when a letter comes not asking for assistance, but telling me how, when they read a particular answer in the weekly column, it was as though the words spoke to them: 'I was able to move beyond the standstill, at last I was free.'

The radio challenge

When I look back on my entry into the world of radio, I must have been crazy! I had somehow ended up working with two of the most controversial, outspoken national radio hosts—it was a baptism of fire!

The words of the producer rang in my ears telling me this high profile presenter wanted a psychic to do a phone reading with him live on air the following day.

'He's leaving the station this week to take up a position with the rival network. His departure has created much media speculation as to how his career will fare, and he needs some direction. Are you available?'

Out of the mouth of babes—or should I say a naive psychic— I said, 'Yes'.

'We'll call you direct, you can give his reading and there may be a chance to give readings to callers. Would you be open to participating?'

'Okay, but all I can do is my best, there are no guarantees.'

I immediately phoned my mother—I was in total panic mode. The man was known as being rude and arrogant; he was acid-tongued and hung up on people.

I said a silent prayer to Spirit that I have the strength, confidence and insight to move beyond his barriers and difficult ways to give this man hope and some light for him to move forward. Taking several deep breaths, I waited for Spirit to come through and give me his messages. I was not prepared for what happened next. I scribbled down all the information given that session. There were pages and pages of notes. Time moved so quickly.

My bed was beckoning, so I leant over, switched off my bedside light and looked forward to a restful night's sleep. However, I wasn't so lucky. I tossed and turned, the thoughts replaying over and over in my mind. He was the king of morning AM radio. His following was massive. What if I was a dud, what if he hung up on me? My fledging psychic radio career would come crashing down. I must have fallen asleep at some point during the night, because I was woken with the sound of the phone ringing.

'Are you ready? We're putting you to air in five minutes—don't hang up. He will also ask you some questions direct—be prepared!'

God, how could I be prepared? I may be a psychic but I'm not a mind reader! I was able to make a quick rush to the bathroom and grab a glass of water before I heard the countdown from the ad break.

'Well, this morning we have Georgina Walker, a psychic, on the telephone. She's going to predict my future. Good morning Georgina. Do you have some psychic vibes for me?'

It was then that an amazing stillness came over me. I wouldn't say I didn't speak quickly, I probably did. But interestingly, there was silence on the other end of the phone line. I thought he must have cut me off, but in fact he was gobsmacked about the infor-mation I had provided. You see, the previous night, I received two Spirit visitors, both related to this man.

I told him: 'There's a man in Spirit who has come to be with you, like an angel or a guide. He tells me he was born in another country and that he protected the borders of that country with a rifle. When he showed me the rifle, it was so long, I was rather surprised at the barrel length. Having migrated to Australia after the war, he hid the rifle among his belongings and secretly brought it here.'

He was amazed. 'Not even my wife knows this story, it's a family secret,' he admitted. 'The man you're talking about is my uncle from Czechoslovakia; he did indeed guard the borders of that country with a rifle like you described. How I know this is that he had it hidden, as it was illegal to hold such a weapon, but one day he showed me the rifle. How could you know this? I'm speechless.'

The second person to come through was a woman who wore an apron, which was tied around her waist. She had a veranda off her house. Each morning she would have scraps of bread in her apron, and would go outside and shake out the crumbs for the birds. My subject acknowledged that this was indeed his aunty.

I think what surprised both of us was that rather than predictions about his future, he had deceased relatives in Spirit wishing to be known to him. I sense he was feeling somewhat isolated, maybe even scared about his future, and his heavenly guides or Spirit helpers were coming through to give him reassurance they were with him in his darkest moments. A lesson I think he comprehended that day is that no matter how high we go, we have our fragilities, but also our guides to support us.

Then the bomb hit. 'Okay, so what will happen with the station and me?'

'They'll live to regret this ever happened. I guess there goes the opportunity of me ever being invited back to this station!'

So much time was taken up with his interview, I never got around to speaking to any listeners, but it did lead to a TV appearance, where I ended up giving impromptu readings to everyone there. Talk about being placed on the spot!

I remember one particular prediction; it was for a well-known sporting journalist and now radio host. At that stage, I didn't know much about her at all. The prediction involved her husband at the time—he would have an incident where she wouldn't hear from him for a number of days. My guides told me not to fear the worst, as he would be fine and no harm would come to him.

After the show she told me he was a journalist, who travelled overseas for assignments. Some time passed and I received news that he and his crew had gone missing in Afghanistan. Yet the prophetic words given that day proved to be accurate—they were unharmed.

Ghostly encounter

The radio station did invite me back. The stand-in DJ wasn't really sold on the idea of psychics and what they could achieve, although he did have some experiences with spooky events in his past. The problem that arose between the two of us was the temperature of the studio. Once we got going he had his job cut out, answering the barrage of calls coming through. I can't recall too much of that particular session, except the most intense coldness I have ever experienced rushed through the room.

With the mics up and a listener on the other end, I am embarrassed to admit, I said live on air: 'It's freezing, why have you turned the studio up so cold?' By this time the DJ was experiencing what I had felt. The colour drained from his face. We both knew we had a ghost or spirit visitor in our midst.

My voice started to go and I started to cough and choke as the presence became more evident and stronger. Worried, the DJ switched to an ad break to see if he could give me some assistance—a glass of water or a pat on the back. We opened the studio doors to allow fresh air to circulate, hoping this would free up any residue from the spirit. It was definitely a male energy. I summoned my own special spiritual law of enforcement by issuing the decree, 'Be gone now, be gone', knowing well Spirit would leave as quickly as they arrived. We regained our composure, telling the listeners what had occurred, and like true troopers it was 'on with the show'.

We found out later in the week that a number of staff at the station had previously had experiences with 'the station ghost'. No-one had told us about that, or I would have been more prepared—sage, salt, holy water, the works.

7

Psychic airwaves

Your time is limited, so don't waste it living someone
else's life. Don't be trapped by dogma—which is living
with the results of other people's thinking. Don't let
the noise of others' opinions drown out your inner
voice. And most importantly, have the courage to
follow your heart and intuition. They somehow already
know what you truly want to become.
Everything else is secondary.
Steve Jobs

ate in 2000 I received a phone call to appear on a national
radio program with the Austereo radio network, 'Hot 30',
which was hosted by Kyle Sandilands and Jackie O. I wasn't
aware then of Kyle's reputation as a 'shock jock'. Later it was
revealed he loved nothing more than to have a celebrity embarrassed or a guest squirm in their seats. Tonight I was to be his
victim—or so he thought.

They presented me with six photos, one was of Tom Cruise and Nicole Kidman and I declared that they would split very soon. Within six weeks my prediction became a reality. As it turned out Kyle took to me and to this day I say to people that he was the one who gave me my start on radio. I was invited to return as a regular.

Working with this team led me to read publicly for some of Hollywood's A-list—one such reading was with John Travolta in his hotel suite while he was in Australia to promote his movie *Swordfish* in 2001. I had already meditated the previous night asking for guidance from Spirit for a knock-out reading that would allow John some prediction or information that normally would never have been known to the general public or even himself. As usual, I cut out a picture of John from a magazine and waited as I knew this method of divination worked extremely fast and gave strikingly accurate accounts of information about the person's past, present and future by keenly opening my perceptive abilities. It's a spin-off from psychometry, where I hold an object belonging to the person I am reading for.

I wrote furiously, wanting the information to flow as Spirit dictated and I became the note taker. I have learnt over the years to allow the material to flow, not stopping to analyse what is being dictated. Should I pause or ponder what's given, my rational brain can kick in and the flow of information can slow or even in some cases stop completely. Reading back what I had written later that evening, I was concerned about how I was going to present the predictions without putting John in a difficult situation by divulging too much or breaking confidentiality. That night during my sleep Spirit showed me the movie *Lorenzo's Oil*—I knew through this example that John would be able to comprehend what I could see.

The interview was to last eight minutes, and I'd be given the last two minutes to quickly get my message across. Walking into John's room, we all shook hands, and as I gazed into his piercing blue eyes, I had the distinct impression that he was reading me!

One team member held eight fingers in the air, signalling the number of minutes we had to conduct the interview. As the time slipped by, the fingers decreased.

It was scripted that when Kyle asked John what his favourite movie was, he would reply *'Grease'*, but instead John looked to me and said: *'Phenomenon*. Not that I want to die, but I would like to live my life that way.' I knew from the film's content that John was indeed psychic.

We were almost out of time but I was able to tell him, 'Due to your early years of suffering [he had been deeply in love with Diana Hyland who was eighteen years his senior and who died of breast cancer] you have been granted fame and fortune as you have a mission to accomplish. Someone close to you, very close, has a male child—I see the movie *Lorenzo's Oil*. Are you aware of this movie?'

John nodded to indicate that he knew of the movie.

'Well, like the movie, this child will be diagnosed with an incurable disease. You will invest much money and eventually find a cure for this disease that in time will save thousands and thousands of people.'

As I pitched the reading, I knew that John would be able to pick up the clue that it was his child, and, yes, he did just that. As I concluded he threw his hands up in the air and said, 'Yes, yes, I knew that was my purpose'. His eyes were shining, and those beautiful white teeth of his exposed an amazing warm smile.

In 2003, it became common knowledge in the media that his son Jett had been diagnosed with Kawasaki syndrome, and at this stage there is no cure. I am convinced this is the mission that the prediction talked about. John is a silent achiever and we may never be told of the amount of money he might personally invest in helping others.

8

Dialling heaven

We are all blessed ones. Heaven is no longer in the
clouds. It is right here, all around us, everywhere; we
must only open our eyes to see it.

Kim Chestney

Jackie O loves the idea that I can speak to dead people. It
is something my regular clients experience as part of their
face-to-face readings. We didn't know how or even if we could
be successful using this format on live radio. One thing I have always
stood firm on is honesty, integrity and saying it how it is. My
mother had taught me to give facts and information first, then ask
questions—that way you would not be soliciting information and
making it fit in. So many people who work in the psychic realm
are not naturally gifted, yet the simple act of looking at someone's
facial features and listening to their voice would be enough to give
generalised predictions. I wanted my gift to be accurate and to
give honest information so listeners could judge for themselves.

Speaking to the other side is not like having a conversation with your best friend. I liken it to speaking on a mobile phone. One minute you have clear reception, the next it fades out. The energies can be strong then soften, as though Spirit is building up their strength to get the messages through. There is truth in the saying 'a picture speaks a thousands words'. Often the energies will hold up a sign—I'll hear a song in my head, see the name of a movie or be reminded of an event I experienced as though that is the example they are trying to show for me to correlate their message. Sometimes more than one energy will come through at a time. This can be frustrating to the client and to me. I liken it to talking to someone on the phone while someone else is also talking to you in the background.

Spirit is just as eager to get messages through as we are to receive them, and when they see a psychic medium working they want to jump in on the party line and give a message to a loved one. It may even be the client's next-door neighbour.

The information comes through so quickly, and in different ways. I can feel—this is called 'clairsentience', or clear feeling—pains in parts of my body that may show where that person had a health condition or how they died, and until I get the information correctly the pain will stay. Sometimes I will taste something—perhaps a particular brand of chocolate, only to find out it was the deceased person's favourite. I may smell a fragrance or a perfume—it could be rose, their favourite flower. I may hear—this is called 'clairaudience', or clear hearing—words, songs and names. And I may also see—clairvoyance, or clear seeing—pictures, photos or names and numbers in my head. Sometimes they are coloured, sometimes they're black and white.

It can be difficult interpreting the signs and signals—it's like asking you to remember what you saw in your favourite television show last night, or recalling a special photo. Those who can remember photo negatives will recall that a seemingly blonde person would be shown as a person with dark hair. This can be a trick the brain plays when interpreting events. Always ask a psychic how they see things. What you see may not be what they see, especially if you are colourblind.

For radio we mapped out a format that to this day is still used for my other segments. The production crew solicited listeners to enrol via telephone. I'd be in a silent studio while they were phoned back. I'd be given their first name only. They'd be telephoned and I'd only ask the name of the deceased they wished me to contact and how old they were when they died.

I would then ask them to think, feel or remember a happy moment or experience involving their beloved. Unknowingly for the client, this small exercise instantly appears to remove the veil of tension, apprehension and fear that they might have originally brought to the consultation. Their barriers are dropped, opening a more positive channel for Spirit to manifest. You know yourself when you're trying to think of a name that has just slipped your mind, the more you force your memory recall, the more it eludes you until finally you relax and the name suddenly pops into your head. The more tense and restrictive the client is, the more energy I need to draw from my own field to break down the barriers they have unconsciously put in place. This then depletes my own energy reserves, leaving me more exhausted after a session.

When they felt they could recall that memory, they were to say aloud their loved one's name three times—three being the very mystical and spiritual numeral that represents Father, Son and Holy Spirit to the western world and in ancient times represented heaven, earth and the abyss. Then I would hang up and write down as much information as Spirit gave me. It's not unusual to start receiving information from the dearly departed while the listener is thinking of a happy moment. It's truly as if they have travelled into the future and knew that their moment was to come, waiting, just waiting for the invisible link from the living world to the afterlife.

After the messages were delivered, I'd be called into the main studio with Jackie and Kyle. Sometimes there'd be ten pages or more of information given and I had to pick the best pieces because I had only two minutes of air time to relay this to the listeners. I liken it to trying to put pieces of a puzzle together, moving them around, seeing how they fit, what fits in where and how to respond to the emotional feelings of the dearly departed trying to convey a message to their loved one—all in a two-minute time frame. Hard going? Yes.

People wonder why I speak so quickly when delivering readings. I'm trying to process all the information given by my six senses. When the information is received from Spirit, it comes through in clairaudient, clairsentient and clairvoyant senses—it's unusual for a psychic to have mastered all three senses, that's why I used the term 'psychic' rather than clairvoyant. I'm trying to process all the information that's being received through these senses at one time, hence speaking rapidly as I interpret the flashes, flickers and feelings before me.

Sometimes listeners can't place a relevant message on air because they lose focus due to the nerves of knowing they're on the radio, and then later the station gets an excited telephone call saying they've just spoken to someone who remembered the information. What a bonus—just a pity we didn't get the feedback on air at the time of the reading.

The messages may sometimes seem disjointed. This is because I have pages and pages of information in front of me, and have to choose what I feel is the best evidence of life after death, being mindful that the DJ needs to insert advertisement and music breaks.

When I'm not reading my notes, I close my eyes and 'feel' Spirit, their energies and their messages, often opening my eyes to see Kyle waving his hand around in a clockwise direction indicating he wants me to wind down for a scheduled break or I have gone beyond my designated time frame.

Radio loves emotion—the station buzzes when an on-air listener shows excitement, screams or, better still, bursts into tears. 'Dearly Departed' left many listeners driving to work in tears as they tapped into the raw emotion of the person having the reading, allowing them to share a private moment with a stranger or an intimate experience that they could perhaps relate to. Often Kyle would hand Jackie and I tissues as tears were rolling down our faces in response to the listener's feedback. It's what makes great radio.

The messages can be very cryptic, and it takes years and years of practice to get the facts interpreted quickly and accurately so the client can glean some sense of what's being given. If the listener's primary sense of relating to the world is through sight, or visual stimuli, then listening to me rapidly passing on information through their auditory senses can be quite difficult for them to absorb there and then.

Liken this to someone who prefers to hear a story being told compared with someone who enjoys reading the story. On radio, we try to paint a picture using visual cues to stimulate the auditory senses with music, dialogue and tonal changes in our voices in anyway we can, so everyone can enjoy and relate to being part of a link to the cosmos—the universal truth that there is life after death.

9

Spirit-inspired synchronicity

Do not assume that divine guidance flows only when
you are in need of help. Guidance continues to flow
whether or not you have problems. It transcends
problems, heartbreaks and traumas, flowing through
dreams and illuminations. Whether guidance comes
during times of tranquillity or trauma, however, it is up
to you to have the courage to acknowledge it.

Caroline Myss

I know there's a divine plan for each soul—we all have a purpose,
and sometimes it's only when we've reached our destination
that we can look back and see the miracle of the wonderfully
woven story of our life's purpose going this way and that way until
the plan has come to maturation. Such was the case with Susie,
an Australian media icon, journalist, author and TV identity.

I've watched Susie's progress in the media over the years with interest, as we share some common ground. When I met Susie, she was gracious and charming, with a charismatic glow about her and an infectious smile.

'Susie—do you realise how much we have in common? We both went to the same high school, and your parents eventually bought the same Caltex service station in the northern beaches that my parents used to own.'

We were both amazed with the coincidences.

Susie had a radio gig that was winding down for Christmas and invited me along as her guest psychic for the very last show. She admitted she was not overly sold on psychics, but she knew listeners loved that kind of thing.

As I fielded live questions from the listeners, and the phones ran hot, Susie seemed more and more surprised at the degree of accuracy; she then asked what I saw for her. I remember quite clearly I saw her in front of a television camera with her own national TV show. When we went into an ad break, Susie turned to me, smiling, and told me she was working on a project around a TV show, and if it came off she would be calling me. Months passed, and I had forgotten all about this prediction when Susie rang, asking me to join the show as the psychic!

A week earlier, I had been visiting Brendan and Latoya, and I was telling them about a series of books about miracles that I just love, written by two Jewish women, that seem to be focused on stories mostly of Jewish families and wonderful synchronicities and events in their lives.

When I returned to Sydney, I kept thinking about my dear friend Simon, who had passed over. His face and name would pop into my head at various times during the day, and I wondered whether he had a message for me. But nothing eventuated...until I hopped into bed one Wednesday evening and looked at my diary. It was June 13 and it was a cold night. I pulled the doona up to my neck, then I heard the song 'Hava Nagilla' as loud as can be! I knew Simon loved this song, coming from the Jewish faith, and I had accompanied him to several functions where it had been played. I started to think, okay, now he's going to give me the message I've been expecting. But no, it wasn't to be the case.

Suddenly a man and a woman appeared in my room—the man stood at the back of my bedroom, in the corner, very still and quiet. As I focused my attention on him, the song changed to a hit from the 1980s called 'Shaddap You Face' by Joe Dolce. I started thinking perhaps this man was an immigrant. My mind kept wandering back to Susie for some reason. I knew her parents were immigrants, but was unsure from where—perhaps Lebanon.

Suddenly it hit me—Simon's birthday was June 21, and that was the day for the filming of the first show, and the show was going to be aired for the first time on June 25, the date Simon died. I wondered if Susie was Jewish. This had to be a message for her. Once I realised this, the visions and messages became more direct. A woman appeared by my bed. She was so excited! She was rather pushy in personality—she came right up to my pillow— then covered my bed with reams and large bolts of dress fabric.

The fabrics on my bed were all different colours, weights and designs. The woman was in a frenzy, saying she hadn't been given enough time to sew dresses for Susie to wear every day, and she'd be flat out making what she could. Then she showed me a ring. It looked like an old wedding ring. She kissed it and placed it on Susie's finger. I wondered—did she perhaps want Susie to wear this ring on the show? I pulled the bedcovers over my head—I just wanted to sleep—but this little woman wouldn't leave me alone. I knew the only way I'd get her off my case was to get up and email all this to Susie.

It was icy cold that night in my office and as I sent the email, the time was 3.17 a.m. Thursday, June 14, 2007. I didn't hear back from Susie over the next few days. I was starting to feel she probably thought she had a nutter on her hands. I dismissed the whole thing, which is sometimes the case with readings.

Filming Susie

When I arrived for the filming of the first show, I was ushered into the make-up room. There was Susie in the main chair having her hair and make-up done by Sherryl, the make-up artist.

After our usual excited hellos, she said, 'There's the ring!' She put her hand up in the air and wiggled her fingers.

'What ring?' was my reply.

'Georgina, the ring—the one you told me about!'

I explained that I'd forgotten all about the email. Smiling, Susie grabbed Sherryl's hand, and said, 'And this is the other ring—Sherryl's my best friend, and I gave her the ring she's wearing. My mother smuggled it out in the war.' On Sherryl's finger was a very large, unusual-shaped natural amber ring. The ring Susie wore was also large, in silver.

She told me her father and had been born in Poland was a holocaust survivor, so the Jewish vibrations were spot on. Her mother was born in Germany of a Polish father and a French mother. Her parents met after the war, and her mother took a silver spoon to a silversmith and had a ring fashioned from it. It would bear her father's initials, with her mother's name engraved on the back.

Susie was just so thrilled with the message. That day she was seeing a dream come true—her very own television show, something she would have loved to share with her parents if they had been alive. Yet through a series of synchronicities she was given the best gift possible—the knowledge that her beloved, dearly departed parents did know of her successes, were so excited and would be with her every step of the day and for weeks to come.

Spirit is indeed grand—they had linked up the vibrations of the Jewish stories, my friend Simon and Susie's parents' appearance in my bedroom. But there is one more, fascinating link—Sherryl told me Susie's mother was a dressmaker.

And upon telling this story to my mother, she smiled and said, 'Gina, Susie's mother made the most beautiful dresses.'

'But how do you know that?'

'She was a really good customer of ours in the fabric shop we bought after the service station.'

10

Enlightenment

I decided that it was not wisdom that enabled [poets]
to write their poetry, but a kind of instinct or
inspiration, such as you find in seers and prophets
who deliver all their sublime messages without
knowing in the least what they mean.

Socrates

L ife never sits still; there is alway something more to learn. I
am a great believer in divine timing, that everything is
uniquely driven in Spirit's time, not our time, and lessons to
be learnt will be placed in front of us at the divine time. By
allowing yourself to be open to the wonders of the world of Spirit,
you will see just how special life can be.

Early in 2006, I had pencilled in late August for a break from
work and an overseas trip—where I didn't know, but I felt sure
Spirit would make me aware of where I was to go. I just knew this
trip would take me overseas, and that I had something to learn.
It was now July, and I had only six weeks before my scheduled

vacation and I still hadn't booked my holiday. The world was out there waiting to be discovered, but I just couldn't get excited about any holiday destination.

Trudy at the local travel agency made some suggestions. 'What about Greece?' she offered, 'or Egypt, perhaps?'

I was a tough client. Each time I saw her she'd give me more inviting brochures to exotic destinations, telling me to go and have a cuppa and a browse and see if they could be possible holiday options. There was nothing that took my fancy, nothing that made my heart sing or that even caused a stirring within my spirit that this was the trip that was 'meant to be'.

With the latest brochures in my bag, I went down to the local shopping mall for that cuppa, and to take in a movie. As I passed the local bookstore I had an overwhelming feeling that I should go inside because there was a book I needed to see. I love to read, and it's not uncommon for me to have two or three books on the go at one time. I often jump from one book and subject to the next as my mood and interest change.

I had a couple of spare minutes before the scheduled movie began, so I followed the internal prompt and went to my favourite section, New Age/Spirituality. Nope, nothing there—read it all or just not interested in what was on offer. Checking my watch, I decided I'd just make the movie if I left now. Turning to walk away, a book literally fell off one of the shelves and rested near my feet. It was actually a little bit spooky, and as I've pointed out to my students, Spirit can and will manipulate books to draw your attention to something you need to learn or know. So I picked it up and scanned through the chapters. There was nothing that leapt out or drew my attention to why I needed to purchase the book, yet I felt compelled to buy it—I knew I was meant to have it.

Reluctantly, I purchased the book and, on returning home that afternoon, placed it on the existing pile of books next to my lounge chair. Each time I tried to read through the numerous pages, it was hard going. I wasn't really enjoying the rhythm or the content, nevertheless I forged on, page after page, when suddenly a name stood out, as though a bright light surrounded it: Roslyn Bruyere. It was the first time I had ever come across this person's name. I was unfamiliar with her and what she was known for. Why was I being drawn to her? I highlighted the name in bright yellow, in case I needed to locate it for some particular reason down the track.

Two days passed and I just couldn't get her name out of my head, so I decided to do a web search. I just love the convenience we have at our fingertips these days with computer technology. I discovered that she was an internationally acclaimed healer, scientist and medicine woman. This led me to her web page, and bingo! She just happened to be conducting a three-day workshop in Cincinnati, Ohio, USA, during the period I had planned for my overseas break. It was enticing—the workshop topic would be the Sixth Chakra, Insight. But it was a long way from Sydney, Australia. I'd need to take the fifteen-hour flight to Los Angeles, then another five-hour flight across to Cincinnati.

I prefer short bursts of travel due to a leg condition, and sitting in confined spaces tends to make me very stiff and I limp off the plane. That's too far, I thought. Cancel that idea. But it kept niggling at me, it seemed too coincidental—the book falling off the shelf, the name jumping out of the page and the workshop at the same time as my holiday break. It was three prods from Spirit—and three is my magical number. When in doubt, wait for three confirmations, and I'd had three . . . Yet I still wasn't convinced that was where I should be spending my vacation.

I had a scheduled appointment to visit Master Zhao several days later. Zhao is the most brilliant Chinese qigong health practitioner I have ever met. Electricity projects from his hands when he heals. He is my battery charger—just like when your car battery is running low and you find an alternative source to give it a boost, I have found with the amount of mental energy I use when conducting readings and Dearly Departed sessions, if I do not recharge my own physical battery, I start to feel very tired and run down. So part of my primary health care is a weekly massage with an energetic practitioner, and several times during the year I visit Zhao for an extra-ordinary zapping of his power into my body.

As I lay on his massage table, Zhao systematically started working on my energy field, balancing, healing and restoring the equilibrium. Suddenly my Asian lady guide appeared, standing to the left of the massage table. Petite in stature, dressed in a heavy red and gold brocade outfit, she bowed and moved closer, positioning herself close to the left side of my head. She always appears ageless, her eyes always twinkle, and her smile seems to melt any worry, pain or uncertainty that I may be experiencing in my life. So I was very surprised that instead of receiving a message of inspiration I was told she would no longer be my spiritual guide, in fact she would be leaving me.

She told me there would be no more access to her as a primary source of wisdom, knowledge and prophecy, and she would be handing over her responsibilities to another spiritual master, who just like she had, would be there to continue the teachings and lessons for my personal development and work on this earth. Racing through my head was, 'I hope this is a dream, maybe it's my imagination'. Yet I knew I was able to analyse her message and reflect on our journey together so what I was experiencing was real.

Years rushed through my head in moments. I recalled when she first appeared to me while I was living in the country and foretold of my connection to come with the 'Land of the Swords', the intended mission she had for me to do the work of Spirit and some glimpses into my personal journey.

Now she was leaving me. I had mixed emotions. I was saddened, almost feeling abandoned, that this special relationship we had was now to finish. I lay in silence, aware that Zhao was still working on my body, when out of the corner of my eye, on the right-hand side, appeared a majestic-looking American Indian chief in full cere-monial dress. He was tall, handsome and proud.

It was then that my lady guide moved to position herself next to my left hip, materialising in her hand what to me looked like a stick or branch. She passed it over my body towards the chief, who was now standing at my right hip. Simultaneously, he moved what appeared to look like a hollow stick over my body towards my lady's stick. They positioned the sticks above my navel then they united and turned into live snakes, intertwining into each other's bodies to form the 'caduceus' which I knew was an ancient astrological symbol. I had never witnessed anything as miraculous as this before.

The chief turned to face me, and I could sense his dark brown eyes penetrating my soul. He then muttered these words: 'Shawnee—White Buffalo.' And with that they both disappeared. I lay silently trying to absorb what I had just witnessed and heard. What did he mean by 'Shawnee—White Buffalo'? Was he indicating he was from this Native American tribe and White Buffalo was his name? My petite Asian guide had never told me her name, I didn't need to know. I always knew and felt her presence.

It was not uncommon to receive a visit from her when I was with Master Zhao. Maybe as I lay in what I often felt was like a semi-trance state, as he worked on my body, she was given effortless access to my mind—as I was rested and still. She had never failed me. All her predictions and visions had manifested as she had shown me. I trusted her guidance, knowledge and wisdom unquestionably. Now she was handing me over, not to another Asian guide but rather an American Indian chief! The only information given was the caduceus and the names, Shawnee and White Buffalo.

I knew that the caduceus was associated with the Greek god, Hermes, who was the messenger for the gods and conductor of the dead, and who had the primal power to heal. And I knew the medical profession had adopted the caduceus as their symbol. I was confused though—I had an ancient Greek symbol and a Native American telling me 'Shawnee—White Buffalo'. What was the link, and how would these connect to my journey ahead?

Researching White Buffalo on the web, I was surprised to find he wasn't an Indian chief, but in fact a Native American legend. The many great tribes of the Native American peoples all had similar stories about the 'White Buffalo'. The Sioux are a warrior tribe, and for example one of their proverbs says, 'Woman shall not walk before man'. Yet White Buffalo Woman is the dominant figure of their most important legend. The medicine man Crow Dog explains: 'This holy woman brought the sacred buffalo calf pipe to the Sioux. There could be no tribe without it. Before she came, people didn't know how to live. They knew nothing.'

The White Buffalo Woman showed the people the right way to pray, the right words and the right gestures. Before she left the people, she told them she would return. As she walked away she turned into a young white buffalo. So for Native Americans the birth of a white buffalo calf is seen as a most significant prophetic sign for their people.

The more I read, the more captivated I became with the story. Some modern commentaries referred to her in more contemporary terms as 'prophetess' or 'psychic'. I could now see threads coming together with my career and a possible link or interconnection to come. On studying the map of the USA to locate the Shawnee nation, I was stopped in my tracks—Ohio. That rang a bell. Wasn't that where Roslyn Bruyere, the world-renowned energy healer and scientist, had a workshop in late August? It was all coming together beautifully. Roslyn was part Native American herself, and also known as a medicine woman. My spiritual quest was unfolding. Cincinnati here I come!

11

Psychic powwow

> At times our own light goes out and is rekindled by a
> spark from another person. Each of us has cause to
> think with deep gratitude of those who have lighted
> the flame within us.
>
> Albert Schweitzer

I registered immediately in Roslyn's workshop. I was surprised—
I suppose I shouldn't have been—to learn that Roslyn's partner,
Ken, was a qigong teacher! It was a double whammy. All I
needed to do then was secure a flight out of Australia to connect
with the workshop. Would I have enough time to link the two
together? Usually, I find that if I'm meant to do something, unusual
patterns fall into place.

The airline had one ticket left at a sale price, and after that
the prices doubled. I was heading off in peak season and I needed
to pay for the ticket within the next two days to secure the seat
and price. But it was a heavy week for outgoings. There were bills
that had to be paid—don't you just love it when they all come in

at the same time? I knew I'd be struggling to pay for the ticket that week along with my other financial commitments. On checking my bank balance, I found the magazine had paid me double, not for one week's column but for two. This was most unusual—or could I say divinely contrived by my new guide!

Nevertheless, it gave me the flexibility to pay for the airline ticket immediately, securing the cheaper airfare and with the bonus of some spending money. I had a mate from Aussie radio, Shorty Brown, who had broken into the comedy world in LA and was living there. Perhaps she could meet me at the airport and we could catch up between flights. I emailed her immediately.

'Sure, but you're going to come and stay with me. Not just overnight, come for a holiday—it'll be a blast! I'll show you the sights of Venice Beach and Hollywood, and you can see my comedy act in Santa Monica. Stay as long as you like. You can get a local flight from LA to Cincinnati no probs from here, just come.'

I was starting to get very excited. This was my first trip to the USA, things had fallen into place very quickly and I felt divinely led. Yet, it still wasn't clear why I needed to go all that way for a workshop. What had Spirit in store for me?

I had forgotten Shorty was such a live wire, and my five days with her were a blur as I was whisked off to the sites, senses and scenes of Tinseltown. Celebrating my birthday at the Hard Rock Cafe, I think I could easily have hidden under the table as the crowd sang 'Happy Birthday'—yes, Shorty had dobbed me in big time!

Cincinnati was hot. Their accents were stronger and my Aussie twang stood out a mile. Steve Irwin, the late great Crocodile

Hunter, had just died, and everyone was keen to connect and speak with anyone Aussie—they loved Steve and he was their hero.

The workshop was amazing—Roslyn was more than I could ever have hoped for. I found it refreshing to sit in a workshop, where no-one knew of my reputation, and just be one of the 'crowd', rather than the presenter. I was pleasantly surprised to discover that many attending the three-day workshop were from medical disciplines—nurses, chiropractors, energetic healers and those working in palliative care. So highly regarded are these workshops, points for attendance are awarded towards their ongoing educational requirements in updating their career qualifications.

One of the incredible women I met at this workshop was Elaine Grohman from Michigan, USA. Pairing up together in an exercise, she was bold enough to say she had noticed my leg condition and would I be open for a healing? After dinner that night, she came to my hotel room and worked on both of my legs; one in particular was very swollen. As she placed both her hands on my legs, gently rotating and massaging the skin, I could feel a tingling under her hands and an emotion welled up within my spirit that reduced me to tears.

The next morning it was as though a miracle had occurred. The swelling had subsided and I could walk with ease! Our friendship was cemented. Over the days, we discussed our lives and our careers. We had similar philosophies and interests. It was most evident to me that Elaine was a woman of great compassion and deep insight. Although her background had been in design and graphic art, now she worked as an intuitive and healer with a passion for palliative care, helping the dying make the transition from this world to the next. How had she been led from one field of endeavour to something so uniquely different?

Elaine's story

Experience is our greatest teacher and at times, through adversity, we will be led to a new understanding or experience that has a profound effect on our current and future lives. For Elaine the passing of her dear aunt would change her life for ever.

Gloria was my mother's younger sister. She was hospitalised as she was in the end stages of diabetes. She was signed on to hospice care and sent home. It was apparent that her time was slipping away. The hospital staff gave a prognosis of two weeks. She lasted almost six. It is truly between God and the individual when their life will end.

On one particular day, my cousin, her daughter and caregiver, was in need of a bit of respite from caring for her dying mother, struggling with the emotional turmoil that care-giving can create, on top of having estranged family members coming into town to be together. Although the dying process can be lengthy, it is a blessing when those that need to make amends are given the opportunity to do just that, to the best of their ability. So, on this particular day, I suggested to my cousin that she take a break and go do something for herself, assuring her that I would sit with her mother until her return.

As I sat in the small room at the bedside of my aunt, I was fairly sure that her time on this earth was rapidly coming to an end. She had been in and out of consciousness that day, and for the most part had been non-responsive. I simply sat by her bed, holding her hand and telling her that if she wanted to go, all would be fine. For quite some time she lay there, seemingly unaware of my presence. At one point, she opened her eyes and said, 'I see my sister.' I said, 'Then honey, you go to her, because she will take good care of you.' That sister was my precious mother, who had died 27 years earlier.

After those words were spoken, she gently closed her eyes. At that moment, I felt a very tangible movement in the room. I can only describe it as a 'whooshing' feeling, gently moving back and forth from side to side. It was a momentary event, but one that would change my life. There was no fan blowing or open window, yet there was a distinct movement. I still can feel the tingle of electricity throughout my body as I recall this movement, intangible yet palpable, in the room. I now know that I was privileged to feel her spirit begin to separate from her physical body. As it turned out, it was just a day or two later that she passed away.

This was a very moving moment for me, since her only sister, my mother, had died when I was thirteen years old, when she was only 47. My aunt and my mother were very close, and I always knew that my aunt was never quite the same after the passing of her dear sister. My world changed forever on that day.

I was very moved by the care that my aunt received, along with the care that the family received. Through the difficult time of impending death, hospice care and the marvellous people that provided it made a lasting impression on me. So much so that shortly after my aunt's death I decided to become a hospice volunteer. From here I enrolled in a two-and-a-half year course of study in Polarity Therapy. It assisted me greatly to understand the energy of the dying process. The most profound understanding was the changing of the human spirit when one has knowledge that their life is coming to its conclusion. The energy of the physical body is beautiful and awe-inspiring, but the unique and mystical spirit and mind can grow and mature in beautiful ways, even as the physical body declines.

I relished in the knowledge of Elaine and others present at the workshop, and was inspired by their great work assisting those who are in the process of making the transition of spirit from this world to the next. This trip had been meant to be. The vision of the caduceus, the medical model, Hermes the conductor of death and White Buffalo married beautifully together.

Through Elaine's knowledge of Native Americans, she felt the visit from the two spiritual masters, and in particular the hollow branch passed over my body by the American Indian chief had more significance than I'd first thought.

'Georgina, American Indian medicine people referred to themselves as "hollow bones", meaning they were like hollow tubes in which energy could pass through to the people they were healing.'

There's a marvellous book called *Fools Crow: Wisdom and Power* by Thomas E. Mails, in dialogue with the great Sioux holy man, Fools Crow. The cover of the book describes Fools Crow this way:

> Frank Fools Crow, Ceremonial Chief of the Teton Sioux, is regarded by many to be the greatest Native American holy person of the last 100 years; a nephew of Black Elk, and a disciplined, gentle spiritual and political leader. Fools Crow died in 1989 at the age of 99.

The book states:

> All medicine persons are hollow bones that Wakan Tanka, Tunkashila and the Helpers work through. In any event, you are being made into a 'hollow bone' or they are acknowledging that you are already one.

> During the workshop, Elaine received a spiritual visitation from a Native American chief who called himself 'Cesar'. Elaine later learnt through a friend who had a guide named Apollo who Cesar was and how important he was to his people. Cesar was of the Adena people who populated the Cincinnati area from 400BCE to about 500CE. They were also referred to as 'Mound People', since they built ceremonial mounds and burial mounds.

'Perhaps Cesar is coming to work with you, Georgina, since he was considered a very revered medicine man to his people,' Elaine said.

It still feels strange to have had a very strong Native American vibration surrounding me in so many directions. As I discussed the complexities of all that had happened and the new vibration with my mum, she reminded me of how I came to be born in a very special hospital, with a unique physician, Dr Rivett. Her story gave me goosebumps!

The Cabarisha connection

Originally my birth was to take place in a public hospital, but my mother had such a bad experience with the nursing staff while visiting, she came home in tears to my father. She told her experience to a couple at the local beach one weekend, and they said there was only one hospital where she should have her baby delivered, and that was Cabarisha. It was a very small private hospital, about 45 minutes drive from my parents' home. It would be expensive, yet my father felt they had been given an answer to their prayers. He was a man of faith, and he and my mother both believed their paths were always divinely led.

An appointment was made for my mother to meet and discuss her confinement with the new doctor at Cabarisha. As she sat patiently in his surgery while he made numerous notations, she observed that on the top of each page of stationery he turned over was a picture of an American Indian.

Mum asked him several times why he used this emblem, and each time he avoided her question. Finally, as I could well imagine Mum wouldn't let up until she found out the reason, he declared, 'This is an Indian, Cabarisha'. Remember, this was back in the 1950s, when there was no New Age openness.

On learning about my birthplace, I discovered Dr Rivett was deeply interested in homeopathy, colour therapy and hypnotherapy; he prepared his own herbal medicines until WWII and experimented in mental telepathy and extra-sensory perception.

Had I gone 360 degrees, from a physical birth with an American Indian guide as the spiritual mentor for a medical establishment and doctor, to an American Indian spiritual mentor guiding and working with me now? Yet, just when I thought I'd had my fill on learning new spiritual wisdoms and insights, Spirit opened another door. All was to be revealed as I travelled in June 2007 to visit my son Brendan and his partner Latoya.

Old Age Wisdom

It was true that I had learnt much about our indigenous Aboriginal population while I lived in the outback, running a drop-in centre for the Aboriginal youth from the local mission. Then when I moved to Dubbo, I gained a reputation for my sensitivity and cultural understanding working with the local Aboriginal community and was offered casual work at the local TAFE college, teaching workplace skills to indigenous people who had recently been released from jail.

Now my breadth of understanding was to incorporate another part of our indigenous culture—to extend and embrace the mystical components that surrounded the Torres Strait Island people, who lived in a cluster of scattered islands off the northern tip of Australia, some reaching as far away as Papua New Guinea. Many had migrated to the mainland of Australia, bringing their cultural beliefs, wisdom and ancestral heritage.

It was on one of these islands that Latoya's mother, Mary, had been born and raised. She was from an island that was known in the past for fierce warriors, headhunters and a tribe who possessed great magical powers that many Islander folk feared.

Both Mary's grandparents were considered 'medicine people'— her grandmother was a healer and her grandfather was a powerful man who had the ability to focus on someone living on another island then conjure and sing a song that would see this person die. It was indeed a practice of magic that you would liken to the magic of Haiti or the West Indies, not associated with somewhere so close to Australia.

I was told stories about the water, sky and land spirits—how some men had the ability to 'shape shift' from man to animal, just as I'd read of particular tribes in the Amazon. I pondered—what was the link between these distant lands and people? Why had this craft gone underground, hidden from western understanding? Mary explained that the majority of Island people were scared to speak of this magic as it was thought that talking about it could in fact attract 'the magic'—which I would describe as 'black magic'.

And with the coming of 'the light' to the Islands, brought by Christian missionaries, the populations embraced Christianity while still maintaining their mystical and ritual beliefs. Their culture was about reading the 'signs' of the land, sea and sky, and their psychic and intuitive ability was highly evolved. It had been and was their gift of survival and it hadn't yet been suppressed like in our western culture.

Mary explained that when Latoya moved away there existed some tension between the two of them that gave way to distance and non-communication. So Mary spoke to her mother in Spirit, telling her in Islander English: 'Mum, Toya not ringing me, what is going on? You go to her and make her ring me.' The request was as simple as that—the belief that Spirit had the potential to deliver such a powerful message.

Latoya butted in then, telling me that just after her mum made the request, she 'lost' her beautiful crystal necklace that she had worn for her graduation. It was expensive and sentimental to her. She looked everywhere in the home and just couldn't understand where it had gone to. It literally had vanished into thin air. Then there was the scary experience of seeing a very dark-skinned spirit-woman in the reflection of her lounge room mirror—she thought someone had died. This happening prompted her to have the courage to ring home and speak with her mother. Wasn't that exactly what her mother had wanted?

It was as though the Spirits were appeased with the open line of communication now existing between Latoya and Mary. Latoya's necklace mysteriously returned! It was found sitting on the sink in the bathroom. Both she and Brendan were stunned. Where did it come from? I remember this event clearly as Brendan had rung me, highly agitated, wondering how this could happen. Mary explained, 'Everything about our family is "signs". If our family doesn't listen to us, the other side will bring them back to us because of the signs they will send.'

There was so much to learn and understand right there in my own country—I sense it is another book in the making. It would now appear my guides were broadening my knowledge and understanding of the ancient ways and beliefs about life, death and the afterlife that make up the Sacred Journey of the soul.

It is true that as a psychic medium I am privileged to communicate with the other side, passing on messages to their earthly loved ones, but now there was much more to consider. What did the souls yearn for prior to their separation from the physical body to heavenly realms? What did they really need from their loved ones here and those already passed over? Could we build a bridge from this world to the next that would allow this phase to be beneficial for all concerned, the departed and the ones left behind?

12

The soul's journey

Dying is not void of the painful emotion we
experience in living. At the same time, dying, like
living, presents opportunity for personal growth and
development. Dying involves choice. And for some
people, the moment of realising that death is
inevitable, that their time is limited, marks the
beginning of a new way of being.

David Kuhl, MD

It was one of those September mornings, somewhat cool, so I
treated myself to the luxury of grabbing a few extra minutes under
the doona. It had been a restless night's sleep, and I was
concerned about my mother. When I visited her the day before,
she sounded rather chesty and was coughing. She was getting over
a bad bout of the flu, so her doctor had said. As I left her house
and was walking up her steep driveway, I kept hearing 'heart,
heart' in my head. She was a robust woman for her 80 years—

she had beaten breast cancer five years earlier, and had bounced back brilliantly.

The doctor had given her antibiotics, having diagnosed a chest infection, so I dismissed the 'message'. Rolling over and checking the bedside clock, I realised I'd fallen into a deep sleep—and there was work to be done. My apartment has bedrooms downstairs and the lounge and kitchen upstairs, and that night I'd left my mobile phone in the kitchen. It must have been several hours later when I walked past my mobile phone and I noticed there had been a message left. It had come through at 4.30 a.m.— obviously I hadn't heard the phone ring. It was from the emergency department at our local hospital saying that my mother had been taken there in an ambulance. She was very ill and I was needed immediately.

The Intensive Care Unit

By the time I arrived at the emergency department, five hours after her admission, my mother had been transferred to the intensive care unit. They'd diagnosed pneumonia, which had subsequently weakened her heart. She was not responding to orthodox treatment. For ten days she went in and out of consciousness. Twice I was told: 'We don't know if she'll pull through. You need to be prepared, due to her age and health, if she goes into cardiac arrest, we won't resuscitate her. Do you understand this? Is there someone we can call to be with you?'

I sat by her bed from early morning until late at night, then after making the twenty-minute trip from the hospital to my home, I would fall exhausted into my bed for a quick nap before returning to her beside. This time my mobile phone lay within easy reach of my hand, should the hospital call.

And sure enough I did receive that ill-fated call: 'You need to come immediately; she has had a huge haemorrhage. We don't know the source and we don't anticipate she will recover.'

But she did. Five weeks later she was out of ICU and into a general ward. She was considered 'a miracle'. Granted she had to go to rehabilitation, and it was a slow process, but nevertheless Mum was grateful for her second, or should we say third, chance of staying alive. Reflecting on her time spent in the ICU, she distinctly remembers experiencing one phenomenon—as she lay unconscious, staff moved around her bed discussing her condition, but she was vividly aware of their conversations. She recalls feeling frustrated, wanting to respond to them, to ask questions, but unable to make any movement or facial expression to draw their attention to her alertness and indicate she was aware of her surroundings and aspects of her health being discussed.

It was during the many hours I spent in ICU that I was able to witness firsthand a number of transitions of the soul from this world to the next. It was an emotional roller-coaster as you walked into the unit. One day there was hope, with families huddled together, rallying when they heard their loved one was making progress, then swinging into a decline by evening as the tide changed and the patient was back in 'critical care'. Obviously, the mood would become sombre and sadness filled the room. The downside of being a psychic, a sensitive, is that you feel and sense more than most people, and at times I could sense and feel that death was in the air.

Some patients had a solo relative or friend sitting by their bed; other cubicles or rooms had a congregation of many people—perhaps friends and family members—all held together by one common thread, their loved one was struggling to sustain life. The suffering for some was in silence, and the expression on their faces said it all; others cried, seemingly in a state of confusion and bewilderment; for others it seemed to be heightened activity, or a sense of peacefulness and serenity. I was perplexed as to why there were such extremes.

On one occasion I noticed a family group standing in front of the swinging doors that led to the ICU—they were trying to convince an anguished woman, perhaps a relative or friend, pleading, begging her, to go inside to visit the very ill person. It was as though that individual had frozen in one spot. It seemed she just couldn't bring herself to take the few extra steps that were needed to push through the double doors that would take her into the ICU and bring her face to face with her beloved.

Sitting with Mum by her bedside was not an option—it was where I was meant to be, yet I couldn't stop thinking of the person on the other side of the doors. For me it was a natural inclination to be with someone I loved and I wondered about the excuses of others, the reasons that justified their non-participation.

'I just can't—I don't want to see him look that way—anyway, what can I do to help?' 'He won't remember me. He's on life support, so why bother putting myself through this stress?' 'I can't help him anymore.' 'It's too late. What's the point?' 'We haven't spoken for ten years. Best I leave it that way and walk away now, before I change my mind.' 'What if he doesn't remember me, I don't think I could live with that, knowing he doesn't know who I am.'

It was most obvious to me that they too were suffering their own pain; a pain that was different from their loved one's, but very real to them. Maybe the process of losing someone so close was tugging away at their own beliefs, their own immortality. Who would be there for them when their time came? Perhaps denial was an easy option—if I don't have to witness this firsthand, it can't be happening and therefore won't happen to them, or me. I wanted to learn 'why'; I wanted to understand the reasoning behind the actions I witnessed.

With so much time on my hands in the unit, I became friendly with the clinical nurse consultants and associate medical staff. It was a rapid time of learning and understanding, not just about my mother's condition and needs, but about the support requirements of the patients and the caregivers. It was felt by the majority of staff that the caregivers who had a faith, be it in God, Spirit or a philosophy, although distressed and sad, would appear to have more resilience, greater coping skills and acceptance that when their loved one died they were on a journey; that there was something beyond this world that was waiting for them—a better place, a place of tranquillity and healing. It gave them a sense of hope that life was infinite.

What saddened the staff the most were the individuals and families who were fractured, divided about how their loved one was to be cared for while they were alive and when they passed over. They placed barriers and conditions on who was informed of the impending death or who could visit their relative—at times denying the dying person's requests to speak with those who mattered most to their heart.

It became evident that for some families the dying person provided a reason to continue to hold onto resentment and bitterness, and to blame, prolonging years of disharmony. Some families could not put away their prejudices, and they allowed their individual emotional states to override the wishes of the person dying. Raised voices could be heard in the patient's room as brothers and sisters couldn't reach a consensus over matters from who would sleep there that night, to who would be informed first or, in the event of death, how the person would be buried.

Sacred moments turned into feuding battlefields. My heart went out especially to those who couldn't move beyond their own position of fear to bid a farewell to their loved one, held in bondage, living in the past, unable to forgive or accept that nothing could be done to undo the past. An opportunity was now present to be able to heal both souls in a time of reconciliation, a time of restoration, yet 'pride' became the number-one killer.

Unfortunately, when this opportunity is missed, later, upon reflection, these people sometimes return to the ICU to seek understanding, counselling and a listening ear. Unfortunately, the staff can't turn back the clock—all they can do is gently refer them to a bereavement counsellor. The opportunity for reconciliation was lost in the moment of yesterday's actions.

What the dying person really needs is to feel unconditional love in an environment that fosters tranquillity and peace, where there exists opportunities to talk about their thoughts, fears and emotions around dying. They need people who will listen, sit with them and be at ease. It's okay to give the suffering person permission to die, reassuring them that their loved ones will be waiting for them on the other side.

13

Sacred dying

The most beautiful people we have known are those
who have known defeat, known suffering, known
struggle, known loss and have found their way out of
the depths. These persons have an appreciation, a
sensitivity and an understanding of life that fills them
with compassion, gentleness and a deep loving
concern. Beautiful people do not just happen.

Elisabeth Kubler-Ross

There were wonderful endings and new beginnings which I
also witnessed in the ICU. Let me tell you the story of one
man and his sacred journey to the other side. I never knew
his name. He was a large-framed gentleman, and he reminded me
of a wise warrior, so for this story I will call him Solomon.

Solomon came from Samoa. He had a mop of salt and pepper
curly hair. He was a gentle giant—I imagine he'd have been a fine-
looking man in his youth. The nurse told me he was 57 and had
suffered a massive heart attack and was not expected to pull

through. He was one of nine children, some living close by, all with large families. This did present a dilemma for the ward, because at times there could be up to twenty people wanting to visit Solomon, so they did it in shifts. Often I would catch up with some of the family members in the television room as we ate our meals together.

They were an animated lot, full of conversation and stories—a family bound together by tradition, faith and belief in God. They were Seventh Day Adventists. They told me that Solomon had been placed on life support until his aged mother arrived in Australia from New Zealand to say her final goodbyes to her son. They believed Solomon should be experiencing life as though he was still at home with them. It was nothing to see them talking to him, singing hymns or native songs, joking, laughing and sometimes eating a snack or two as he lay there peacefully in his bed. His wife would brush his hair and talk to him as though his eyes were open and he understood each word.

One morning I came in and there was a delicious smell of coconut oil filling the ICU. I then saw Solomon's wife massaging his limbs with this fragrant oil, no doubt a familiar smell from their tropical home. She seemed to coo words of love and comfort as she tenderly stroked his arm and massaged his large biceps. He was being pampered, he was being loved. Nothing was held back. They even snuck in his grandchildren—although not allowed—to kiss him and have little conversations with their grandfather. They all knew it was a waiting game, until his mother arrived and the support system would be switched off.

He was adored to the final moments. It has been scientifically proven that our hearing is the first sense in our mother's womb to be developed and it is also our last sense to leave us, and quite fitting that Solomon would be sung to and talked to as the soul would hear and acknowledge the vibrations, the messages and the intent. There was such reverence and respect as they tended to his needs. His body and his soul were feeling the power of love through touch. It became a dialogue between the patient and the carer.

Finally, after a number of days, his aged mother arrived. As she sat next to his bed holding his hand, she too talked to him, and for me, the onlooker, it appeared she believed he heard every word. I was not privileged to be there when Solomon's soul left and moved on, but my mother, who had the adjoining room, said there was a special service around his bed that night, where family gathered, prayers were said and songs sung. She overheard a gentleman telling Solomon he was now free to go on his journey over the water. We presumed this was when the life support was turned off. Solomon, I sense, would have felt blessed, adored, comforted and reassured that his exit from this world and entry to his heavenly realms were indeed a sense of celebration, his sacred journey to his Lord had commenced with his loving family by his side.

Not all passings are as beautifully orchestrated and lovingly supportive as Solomon's. The final moment for the soul to leave the body can well be manipulated and controlled beyond our human experience and understanding. Over and over again I have had clients tell me: 'I just went out for a cup of coffee, and she died while I was gone. Why did she do that? If only I had stayed, I could have been there until the very end. I can never forgive myself for being so selfish.'

I have learnt from many years of communicating with the other side that what seemed a lonely, isolated departure, with no loving support standing by, in some cases had been the will of the beloved; it had been their preference, their choice of departure, at that very moment. Many dearly departeds who have suffered greatly towards the end, in pain and much discomfort, felt they would have liked to pass over much sooner; however, they could hear or were aware of the neediness, clinginess and the cries of their loved ones. Some bargained with God to save them or keep them alive while their loved ones pleaded for them not to go, to stay a little longer. They felt an obligation to sustain themselves for the sake of their earthly loved ones.

Then a window of opportunity presented, and in the stillness and quietness a choice was given: 'Come now—I am waiting for you.' Some spoke of a vision or feeling of a divine visitor, some saw an angel, a deceased parent or loving relative come to collect them. They felt immense love and lightness to their being. They knew without reservation that now was the time to depart. There were no regrets; it felt right. They were no longer caught between two worlds; they felt free at last!

Others expressed that a number of days before their passing they had been aware of a heavenly presence in their room. Some had conversations with these heavenly visitors while others chose to listen. The loving sensations that emitted from the heavenly visitors took away any fear of dying. This unique time had prepared them for their coming sacred journey, where there would be a release, as beautiful as the day they left their mother's womb to commence another life, another journey. Now, yet again, they were being prepared for the journey home. Their life had come full circle!

Through their guidance I have learnt a new insight—a revelation that loved ones who passed at the hands of others, for example in the case of murders, drownings and even accidents, expressed that they felt no pain at the time of impact. Some actually said they saw the event as it was occurring, played out in slow motion in a feeling of dislocation from their physical body. They felt a floating sensation, as though they were in an altered state, giving them access to view what was happening to them at that point on the earthly plane. They could feel no pain, no terror; they were just observers. They likened it to sitting in their favourite chair and watching a movie on television. I sense this was when the soul started to pull away into another dimension.

I know scientists agree that energy cannot be destroyed; it can only be transformed. These experiences describe the soul transforming and preparing itself for the next life—the afterlife!

14

For the love of Mary

What is a friend?
A single soul dwelling in two bodies.
Aristotle

Sometime after Mary's husband died, she moved into a brand new townhouse complex, giving her personal security in a close-knit community where there would be help close by if she ever needed it. Mary did have some distant relatives; however, she was fiercely independent and somewhat private, so the thought of losing control to pestering relatives went against the grain.

A 'lover of life' would describe her perfectly. Even though Mary was in her late eighties, nothing would stop her getting out and about—her regular daily walk to the shops, or donning a sarong and having a dip in the ocean with squeals of joy. I admired her adventurous spirit. She even encouraged Tom, her next-door neighbour, who was in his seventies, to join her in a basic computer course. She was keen to learn how to navigate the internet.

Mary was childless so Tom was like the son she never had and he, his wife Lolita and their three children became her family. It was through their daughter, Kerrie, my best friend, that I became acquainted to this tiny energy ball of a woman. We would meet at Christmas, birthdays and special events. Lovingly, Kerrie and I referred to her in conversation as 'Old Mary' to avoid confusion between several other people with the same name.

Returning from a trip to Canada and Alaska, Mary excitedly told me how she had been wooed on a cruise ship by a Texan widower in his early nineties—he was phoning her regularly and had proposed marriage over the telephone. He had even sent her an engagement ring in the mail. 'What should I do, Georgina? If I marry him I'd be leaving Australia, my home and my little dog. What do you think?'

Weighing up the pros and cons, she decided to decline the offer—after all, her garden was her pride and joy, and it couldn't be abandoned after all her hard work.

Mary had one vice, the love of cigarettes. 'I've never been sick a day in my life,' she would constantly tell us. I presume she was trying to justify her vice by reminding us that she was 'fit as a mallee bull', as the saying goes.

My last great memory of Mary was a Christmas Day spent at Kerrie's home. We sat out in the bright Aussie sun among the beautiful gum trees. Mary was in fine spirits, laughing and making jokes about Lolita wanting to pull out or prune the climbing rose bush Mary had planted for Kerrie some two years earlier. Kerrie had christened the bush 'Mary Rose'. Mary was insistent that the rose bush would regenerate in its own time, but it did look a tad sad.

Several months passed and Kerrie told me that her father, Tom, was concerned that Mary hadn't been quite herself—not the bright, bubbly character we had all come to love and adore—and she was sharp, a bit cranky and sometimes more distant than usual. Her back was giving her pain, and for the first time in her life, so she said, she had to visit the local doctor. A random X-ray revealed a spot on her lung. She had to see a specialist for further tests, and return for those test results a week later.

Tom became her taxi driver, and accompanied her into the specialist's surgery for the verdict. The ill-fated diagnosis, 'You have lung cancer', was delivered, and the prognosis was not good. 'It's estimated you have only four to six weeks to live,' the doctor said.

Determined to beat any obstacle placed in front of her, she threw away her cigarettes and stopped smoking—yes, after all those years. Mary commenced chemotherapy within two days. As it does in most cases, the chemotherapy took its toll on her energy and vibrancy. She constantly vomited, and progressively became weaker and frailer. I sense she realised there was no turning back, that the illness would eventually take her. True to her spirit, she had organised her life, the will, the burial service, and what was to happen to her dog and assets.

Mary's final wish was to die at home. The home-care service had modified her two-bedroom unit, as walking upstairs to her bedroom was now an impossible task. Her laundry had been converted into a shower and her lounge room was now to be the bedroom. Discussion had occurred about hiring a part-time nurse so she could have some practical assistance in the home. However, when the palliative care team met to discuss her leaving the hospital, there was a mixed consensus as to how she would cope without 24-hour care. There was one particularly strong-willed nurse who felt Mary should not be allowed home. So Mary's request to die at home was denied. She was to spend the rest of her living life in a palliative care facility. With no goodbyes to her beloved dog and majestic garden, it would be a solitary existence.

The news was devastating—she had organised so much in her life, and done so much on her own, then her own free will had been taken from her. From that moment, she lost the will to live, declining rapidly, refusing to see anyone but Tom's immediate family who were frequent visitors to her bedside. She had gone from a robust, energetic woman to a tiny bundle of skin and bones. Tom was stricken with grief, and could only manage to sit with her for brief moments. It broke his heart to witness his dear friend so incapacitated, and visiting became agonising.

Kerrie's son Joshua and his girlfriend visited Mary on one Saturday night. Kerrie lived a two-hour drive away in the Blue Mountains and had a young baby, Olivia-Charlotte, to care for, so she needed to plan her visits around the feeding and sleep patterns of her baby. After all, if they scattered the visits between family members, Mary wouldn't be so lonely or so fatigued talking with them. But on the Sunday, Kerrie had an overwhelming feeling that she must go immediately to see Mary—something wasn't right.

Peter, her partner, tried to talk her out of making the two-hour trip—it was getting late and she had planned to visit the following week anyway. But so strong was the internal prompting and feeling that Kerrie was experiencing, she decided to leave washing her hair and putting on her good clothes—she just threw the essentials for the baby in the car and she was about to drive herself to Sydney when Peter reluctantly agreed to drive them both to the hospice.

As they entered Mary's wing, the nurse on duty seemed relieved, saying, 'I'm so pleased she has a visitor'. Kerrie and Peter sat on opposite sides of Mary's bed, each holding her cold little hands. Mary squeezed Kerrie's hand, acknowledging her presence. It was such an emotional time. Kerrie has what I would call a photographic memory—she remembers everything in fine detail. So as she sat next to Mary, she relived the many conversations and stories Mary had shared with the family over the years of their friendship. These were of her childhood, the animals she had nurtured and cared for, her happy marriage and the joy of hearing about Olivia-Charlotte's birth.

Kerrie described Mary's garden to her—something she adored and would relish hearing about—and the flowers that had bloomed while she'd been away. Kerrie told her that it was okay to go now; her husband, little animals and parents on the other side were now lovingly waiting to receive her. Then it happened—Mary's tiny cold hands became very warm, and within minutes her whole body was burning hot. Kerrie and Peter were alarmed and called for the nurse.

'This is a most unusual change of events. I feel the time is very close for Mary to leave,' the nurse said.

Kerrie sensed Mary's soul was rising, ready to depart. Olivia-Charlotte, the baby, was becoming restless, as all little ones do, and although Kerrie and Peter wanted to stay longer, what was a peaceful, tranquil setting was now becoming rather noisy and disruptive. So Peter, Kerrie and Olivia-Charlotte gently kissed Mary goodbye, and within several hours she had passed, with the nurse by her side.

The Sign of the Rose

Mary's passing was not completely as she had wanted it—she was denied the right to pass away at home, so those closest to her brought her home to her in stories, flowers, familiarity and love. Kerrie and Mary had shared the same beliefs about life after death, and that those departed can and will give those they love 'signs' they are near. So Kerrie made a decree to Mary: 'If you are around me, I want to see twelve rosebuds—more would be even better—on your Mary Rose bush in the next two weeks.'

Well, Kerrie didn't get twelve rosebuds—in fact, the Mary Rose bush sprouted sixteen buds! Kerrie received the message that indeed Mary was around her. Who would have thought a rose bush, living but not thriving and rather sad looking would suddenly come into bloom? Mary was true to her word that the bush would regenerate in its own time.

As I was writing this story, I rang to check some of the details with Kerrie, and she was over the moon. 'Something miraculous has just occurred,' she said. Several days earlier, she'd been going through a personal crisis, and had been asking the universe for some guidance. She felt she needed something to snap her out of her depression.

'If only I could see an owl, that would make me feel better,' she said. Kerrie had been captivated with owls since seeing the movie *Harry Potter*. She stepped outside that evening to have a cigarette. The night was very cold, so she wouldn't be spending much time out there. Suddenly, from her right side, an owl swooped down and landed on the railing of her veranda, just a metre or so in front of her—within arm's reach, if she had wanted to touch it. She was stunned! She had never had an owl sit on her veranda, so close—previously she had seen the occasional one sitting up in the gum trees, but so close, never. She wanted to Peter to come and look, but felt that if she called out she'd scare the owl, so she stood motionless.

Then it flew and sat on the tiniest little branch of the Mary Rose bush. So small was the branch that not even a sparrow would be able to support itself on it. The owl fell, shook itself, and then walked some distance onto the cemented area in front of the veranda. It cheekily hopped over to four empty ceramic planters, and peeked inside them as if to say, 'Hey, there's work to be done! These are empty. Get moving, what are you planting in here?' Then the owl turned to face Kerrie, tilted its head to one side as though it was acknowledging her, waited a few moments, and then flew away.

'It's a message, Kerrie,' I said. 'Remember how the owls in *Harry Potter* brought the messages to Harry, rather than in the post?' I believe the owl was Mary, or from Mary, after all we called her 'Old Mary', and reference is always made to the 'Wise Old Owl'. 'You'll be fine, Kerrie,' I said. 'The owl is telling you all will be well.'

Devotional love

Animals bring messages, sometimes I believe heavenly inspired. Amanda's dad had been gone for just three days and she was sitting on her veranda, pondering the forthcoming funeral service when suddenly a sulphur-crested cockatoo flew down and sat on the wooden railings. The beautiful yellow feathers of his head were open in full array, resembling a beautiful gold aura, like you see around the great masters of Jesus, Mohammed or Saint Germain. Tilting his head to one side, his eyes seemed to peer straight through her. She had never had a bird like this come to her home.

There were some leftover biscuits from her morning tea on the little table by her chair. Very carefully placing them in the cup of her hand, she gradually moved out of her chair and gingerly walked towards the bird, presenting the small offering. She was surprised as the bird moved closer to her and accepted the morsels.

A flood of childhood memories flashed in front of her, taking her back to her parents' home in the mountains.

Amanda remembered how the cockatoos would gather in the trees surrounding their home in the late afternoons. Their squawking was deafening, silenced only when her dad ventured out with trays of his traditional mix of moistened bread and honey, one of their favourite afternoon treats. She remembered how her father would lovingly and patiently guide her young hand towards the perched cockatoos, sitting on the side fence. It was how she had learnt to overcome her fear of birds. They had seemed so large compared to the small stature of a seven-year-old child.

Had her father sent this bird? Or better still—was this bird her father? Amanda may never know. Within her spirit she felt that the unexpected visitor was divinely sent to remind her of a fear she had learnt to overcome with the aid of her father's presence. Now in spirit, he could still reach out and guide her through this new fear surrounding death.

There will be some people who have not experienced the devotional love of a pet and will never be able to comprehend your depression and sadness at the loss of your beloved pet. You may suffer in silence. Their passing may trigger a memory of someone else you have lost, and the flood of emotions may well rush back. At this time you may wish to choose some of the examples I have used in the chapter 'Life is a Celebration' to guide you through this process. It will take time to work through the emotional rollercoaster you are experiencing. Don't compare your time in grieving to that of a friend. We're all at different stages. However, there's one thing I can guarantee—time does heal!

Many of you will be wondering what has happened to your special mate. It's only natural to want to know if your pet is with familiar faces or people they knew when they were alive. In one Dearly Departed reading, I remember seeing a particular dog sitting quietly and contentedly on the feet of their loved one, only to be told afterwards that the dog belonged to the next-door neighbour and was always chasing their cats! Maybe the dog chose them because they were a familiar person—it certainly looked content. Perhaps theirs was a karmic lesson of tolerance and forgiveness that needed to be worked out between the two.

Nevertheless, your beloved animal will be linked with familiar individuals on the other side. They are not alone!

15

Time to go

And it is in dying that we are born to eternal life.

St Francis of Assisi

Solomon's last days became a profound spiritual experience for all concerned. His family's ritual became a sacred act of service, allowing his soul to be nurtured with grace and dignity as he moved from this world to the next. And as for Mary, her beloved friends' end-of-life vigil was shared with her through comforting stories, prayers and gentle touch.

There are also some dearly departed souls who choose to make the final farewell themselves—appearing to their loved ones in dreams and visitations. This happened to Diane. Diane just adored her Papa Alfred and Nanna Florence. The extended family all lived within half an hour's drive of each other, which enabled Diane to spend much of her time growing up with her grandparents. She was especially close to her grandmother. Diane enjoyed hearing stories about when Florence was a girl, and she would read storybooks to Diane. She felt treasured and adored.

As Diane matured into a woman and became a mother herself, they both realised they had something more in common. They both shared a great love and interest in the supernatural world and all things psychic. Diane was devastated when she learnt that Papa Alfred had been rushed to hospital suffering from a severe stroke. At the age of 82 the prognosis wasn't good—he could pass away at any moment.

Florence knew Alfred was made of tough stock, and if anyone could prove them wrong he would. She refused to believe he was going to die. The family rallied around his bedside, and the priest had been called to give Alfred the 'last rites'. The hospital staff suggested the family go home for some rest—they'd be notified if there were any significant changes. Florence was still in a state of denial, refusing to believe that her beloved husband was on the brink of dying, so she went home with the rest of the family to freshen up. A lovely bath was prepared for her, and Diane and her parents quickly showered and dressed, as they knew the hospital may call at any moment. Diane's parents decided to return to the hospital while Diane stayed with Florence, to keep her company and watch over her as she had complained in the hospital and since returning home of funny pains in her stomach.

Due to the rush to the hospital, Florence had missed taking her daily dose of laxative, and asked her daughter to buy some for her at the local chemist the following day, believing this was the reason for the pains in her stomach. Diane and her dad had recently attended a meditation course, and both had practised a guided imagery meditation recorded on a tape. They had each purchased a copy. Diane felt that if she could talk her nanna into doing this meditation, she'd feel calmer and at peace, and perhaps her stomach pain would settle.

She knew where to locate her dad's cassette, and made the suggestion to Florence. First she gave Florence some reiki healing then settled her comfortably on the lounge before switching on the cassette tape that played a meditation called 'The Sanctuary'.

About three-quarters of the way through the meditation, Florence put up her hand and said to Diane, 'I have just seen my mother and heard her voice, she's calling me Florrie. Doesn't it mean when you see this and somebody calls you that you're going to die?' Diane explained that she didn't know what it meant, and tried to get Florence to focus on positive things—that her husband was going to be all right and if not, there would be people in the afterlife who would be there to look after him and make him cups of tea, and not to fear living by herself as she knew she would be welcome to stay with her daughter and son-in-law.

Florence wasn't comforted by this, as she loved her home and beautiful garden. Diane suggested they return to complete the meditation, but Florence's mind was elsewhere and she asked if they could leave it for the time being. She was concerned that if her beloved Alfred died, who would make him his sandwiches, get his pyjamas ready, roll down the bed and just basically take good care of him, like she had.

Just then Diane's parents returned from the hospital saying that Alfred was 'holding his own', and if he was still going, they would leave early the next morning to visit him.

Florence was feeling very tired, still with the funny pain in her stomach, so her daughter put her to bed in the spare room, and the last Diane remembers of Florence was of her sitting up with piles of cushions behind her back, her daughter sitting on the side of the bed giving her a cup of tea. Diane kissed her nanna goodbye as she left for her own home for a rest and a change of clothes.

When Diane arrived home, her son was curled up asleep next to his father in their bed, so she decided to sleep the night in her son's bed. Turning off his bedside light, she fell into a deep, deep sleep.

Suddenly, she awoke to the bedside light switch on, and heard Florence say, 'Diane, Diane—wake up'. Diane was exhausted, she didn't want to be rude, but felt she just couldn't totally wake up— she hoped she was dreaming.

Then her nanna touched her on the shoulder, and in a rather offish tone Diane said, 'Oh Nan, what is it?' She wondered to herself what Florence was doing in her son's bedroom. Maybe the whole family's here to tell me Papa has died. Finally she asked her nanna, 'What are you doing here?'

'I must leave you,' Florence replied.

'What do you mean?'

Florence smiled and said, 'Good night Dolly, I must leave you.' She learned forward and kissed Diane.

Still feeling disgruntled, Diane thought to herself, 'Whatever, I'll see you in the morning.'

Then she heard Florence say, 'Goodbye PK.' Dolly and PK were pet names her nanna called her. She had a drawer full of two types of chewing gum, PK and Juicy Fruit, and whenever Diane left Forence's house she'd affectionately say, 'Goodbye PK', and Diane would say, 'Goodbye Juicy Fruit'.

Diane went back to sleep, only to be woken by her father opening the bedroom door and switching the light on. Diane asked her father if Papa had died.

'No, Diane, I have some sad news—Nanna has died. She died while your mother sat on her bed. She said she had a pain in her stomach, took a deep breath, put her head to one side and she was gone. You need to come back to the house, everyone is there.'

By the time she arrived at her parents' home, the doctor had been and gone, declaring Florence had died from a burst aorta, the police had left and Florence's body had been taken to the morgue. Diane was devastated as she had only spoken to her nanna several hours before at her parents' house, where they shared a meditation together, and she wanted to say goodbye to her physically.

Several of the family members escorted Diane to the morgue where she saw Florence for the last time. Diane really felt she needed to see her in the flesh, only then would she believe Florence had really died and the visit from her was a spiritual visitation. Her soul had come to bid farewell especially to her, something Diane would be able to treasure for the rest of her life. The visit did in fact make Diane feel better. It was now obvious to the family that Florence knew Diane would be very distressed and made a special effort to say goodbye.

Alfred lay unconscious in the hospital for another six days. The family members visited him frequently—some gave him reiki, and others told stories of events and special days that would be familiar to him. One particular day Diane leant over to her papa, kissed him on his forehead and whispered in his ear that Florence had died. 'She went to make plenty of cups of tea for you. She has some beautiful cakes—your favourite. She was worried that if you went, there would be no-one to take care of you. Now you have her waiting for you—it's okay to go to her.' Alfred passed away several hours later, in his sleep.

16

The twin sisters

To live in the hearts we leave behind is not to die.

Thomas Campbell

May and Ivy were twin sisters, not identical, but close in ever other way. They lived in close proximity to each other, their children grew up together and they shared their Christmases and other special days—their bond was inseparable. Yet Ivy passed away some twenty years before May, leaving this world on Mother's Day. It was a tragic loss for May.

In the following years, May suffered breast cancer, and then a diagnosis of Parkinson's disease followed. She managed well for quite some time, with a loving husband, supportive daughters and grandchildren, but finally she needed to be hospitalised as the condition had progressively worsened. She needed intensive hospital care as her small-framed body shook from morning until night. The doctor said it was as though the poor woman was racing a marathon every day of her life.

The family made her room as comfortable and as homely as possible, surrounding her with familiar photos, and she was fortunate enough to be able to view a little garden from her window. How long she would be able to sustain her existence was not known, but I strongly suspect the infinite bond between the twin sisters surpassed all barriers of communication, for May passed away, on Mother's Day, the same day her twin sister had passed away many years before. Twin sisters born with the same birth date died on the same special day.

Is there something greater, beyond our own understanding, that Spirit can manipulate their time of passing? Is there a greater plan, in this case a legacy for those they left behind, that two women who entered this world together would now leave for their children and grandchildren an anniversary date that no-one could forget?

How do you say goodbye to the ones you love? Is there a right or wrong way to be present, not to be present, what to say and what not to say? Maybe some of the following suggestions could be food for thought.

End-of-life rituals

In our society, many people have lost touch with the spiritual aspect of death and dying. It's a subject that's usually taboo, but may resurface when someone you love is dying; placing you in a position of contemplating what is needed to make the transition peaceful from this world to the next.

As the Bible says, 'Ask and ye shall receive'—seek out assistance. Don't feel you need to shoulder this difficult time by yourself. There are people and organisations that have been especially trained in Sacred Dying—your hospital chaplain, minister, priest or rabbi may be your first port of call. There are organisations which can help you, such as the Sacred Dying Foundation which has wonderful literature available for downloading from the internet on www.sacreddying.org. It may be the starting point to assist opening up dialogue with other family members as to how you are to handle the coming days. Something to consider is a vigil, described below by the Sacred Dying Organisation.

What is vigiling?

Vigiling is primarily concerned with providing spiritual presence for the dying, and can include the act of praying, talking, and/or performing rituals. A vigilier accompanies a person from life to death, while providing whatever is necessary to make the transition peaceful. With Sacred Dying, the end-of-life transition becomes an opportunity to bring reconciliation and acceptance to the dying and their loved ones. In the vigiling process, you may consider incorporating into your daily activities time spent sitting together, talking, listening and, at other times, in shared silence. There may be opportunities to read inspirational texts, or provide healing touch through massage, holding hands or gentle strokes. Setting a comforting mood through ritual can also be considered.

End-of-life rituals can help a person to die not only a peaceful death but also a sacred death. The Sacred Dying Vigil can include anything from a formal religious ritual to something simple and personal. These rituals can aid in a more meaningful passing and can include beautiful poetry and particular readings, the aid of music, and setting the mood with candles to allow serenity and peace to enter the surroundings.

There will be no right and wrong way as you 'feel' your way through the dying process. The family and friends of Solomon, Mary, Alfred and Florence chose to honour their loved ones' final days in uniquely different ways, yet each process, each action assisted in building bridges from this world to the next.

17

Blueprint of the soul

Soul is at home in the deep, shaded valleys,
Heavy torpid flowers saturated with black grow there,
The rivers flow like warm syrup.
They empty into huge oceans of soul,
Spirit is a land of high white peaks
and glittering jewel-like lakes and flowers,
Life is sparse and sounds travel great distances,
There is soul music, soul food, and soul love…
People need to climb the mountain not
simply because it is there,
But because the soulful divinity needs to
be mated with the spirit.
Tenzin Gyatso, the 14th Dali Lama

J ust for one moment, I want you to turn the palms of both
your hands up. First look at the left palm, then your right
palm—notice that the lines on the hands differ from one
another. I recall having my palms read by one of Australia's leading

palmists, Paul Fenton-Smith. He looked at both hands in great detail, his eyes moving backwards and forwards over them, carefully studying the shape of each hand, the lines and marks that formed a 'map' of my life, past, present and to come.

I was stunned with the accuracy of detail he was able to divulge without knowing too much about my growing-up years. He explained to me that my non-writing hand, which for me is my left, was like a profile of my character and potential, and it doesn't change much with age. However, for my dominant hand, my right, the lines would change and evolve in time to demonstrate what I had achieved and other significant events around health, family and occupation—amazing!

Literally our future lies in our hands. I reflected—if we are born with road maps of past, present and future in our hands, then there truly exists a blueprint of the soul from one life to the next, a tiered effect of past vibrations of who I was to who I am and who I will be in the future.

Each religion of the world has a similar philosophy, a belief that life is eternal, that we go on to live somewhere else—whether it's heaven or the afterlife—somewhere eternal, one day to be 'born again' to spiritually evolve and move forward while reflecting on where we have been—our past. It was the Egyptians who were the first to believe that the soul was immortal. With similarities documented in the spiritual traditions of the Greeks, Romans and Celts, the eastern cultures refer to this as reincarnation. I am in wonder at how beautifully Mother Nature has orchestrated rebirthing in the plant kingdom with perennial plants—bulbs planted in rich soil, sprout, grow, blossom, wilt, then recover and rebirth next season, they too fulfilling their genetic blueprint.

Science has proven through the study of human DNA the accuracy of correlating our biological parents—they can even pinpoint which continent our ancestors came from centuries ago! So too our souls come with their own DNA memory bank of past, present and future.

The majority of people will have experienced meeting someone for the very first time, and perhaps the hairs stood up on the back of their neck, they got a quiver down their spine or they felt they had known them a lifetime—there was an instant connection. My friend Jules met her husband at a conference like I had predicted— they literally bumped into each other as she stepped out of an elevator. Later he told me that when he saw her, he just thought 'there goes my future'. He didn't know where that came from— it was just a knowingness, a meaningful coincidence.

I sense that random events and meaningful coincidences are spiritual forces guiding our destinies along the soul's blueprint. I suspect Jules and her partner once again had connected at a soul level—a soul connection from a previous incarnation. Maybe they would achieve perfection in this union, fulfilling their karma and reaching nirvana, never to return to this earth again. Are you still searching for your soul mate? You could well be waiting a number of lifetimes.

We have been led to believe that there exists a true happy-ever-after love story just waiting to complete you—someone who is perfect and brings you a lifetime of bliss and happiness. In fact, what the soul is calling for is completion—completing this lifetime's karmic ties. I sense it is a much softer option to believe in 'soul connections'. If you're so hooked on the notion that there is only one love out there who will truly make you happy, you'll be waiting a long time. Soul connections are not necessarily lovers—they come in all shapes, sizes and sexes.

Your soul will vibrate to an energy that will let someone special or even difficult enter your life and allow your soul to learn what it needs at that particular moment. It may be your next-door neighbour; the difficult, demanding schoolteacher who pushed you to your limits to see you on your career path; the hard, critical father who eventually led you to needing psychotherapy—why? Only to see you would make a great psychotherapist yourself as you learnt to resolve the issues of the past and by doing so open your heart to find a new love connection.

Gifts, whether painful, shameful or beautiful, are of the soul connection kind. Our soul connections are red flags on our map of life, bringing to our attention what we need to experience and work through as we continue along the blueprint of our soul.

Soul birthing

Those who have been around children often say: 'She's been here before—there's a certain knowingness,' or, 'It's like looking at an old man. He's definitely been here before.' I believe those words that pop into your head are very prophetic. Unknowingly, they are recognising a quality of an old soul. It has been debated for centuries as to the exact moment when the soul activates or descends into the unborn body. Some believe it hovers around and integrates at the time of the 'quickening', when the mother feels the first movements of the baby in her uterus. Some say it's at the time of birth.

Ask any mother who has carried several children in pregnancy, and she will compare the personalities of the unborn babies. 'This one will be a calm baby,' she may say. Or, 'He has more character than my first.' Perhaps it's, 'This one loves the music I play, he's dancing inside me,' or, 'This little one has been here before—I just know it.'

Mothers do know—they sense the qualities of the soul they carry. They may have vivid dreams about the nature and character of the child. They give the unborn child a name—they don't really know where the idea came from, they just thought of it. It's not a name that would be familiar to them or perhaps that they've even discussed with their partner—it just felt right. And they know if they're carrying a boy or girl child.

If you can accept the notion that a soul chooses its parents so that it can understand and learn lessons in the new life, then for those of you who have grieved over your decision to terminate a pregnancy, or have experienced a miscarriage or a still birth, having this knowledge that these little ones knew their time in this life would be somewhat short may be able to lessen the blow. This time maybe they were to be the teachers to the parents, gently touching their emotions and pointing them in a new direction of their souls' purpose.

There are some tribes in Africa who, at the time of the death of their child, actually place a cut or burn on the skin or break a bone to disfigure the body, believing that when the child reincarnates the markings or disfiguration will reveal who they were previously. It gives a whole new meaning to birthmarks and congenital deformities if we adopt the belief that our bodies will hold a key or clue through memories of a scar or physical manifestation of abnormalities that may pinpoint a previous reincarnation.

One of my children has a very unusual brown birthmark splattered on his chest. I've often puzzled at this. Could it have been the entry site for a bullet or sword? How could this be proved—that there existed a correlation between this mark and his past lives?

Dr Brian Weiss, head of psychiatry at Mount Sinai Medical Center in Florida, US, and author of *Same Soul, Many Bodies*, has done much work with past-life therapy, and has been able to retrieve detailed information of individual past lives. He believes the choices we make now will determine the quality of our life when we return, and that a person's remembrance of a past life may be relevant to a problem in this life.

There also now exists overwhelming evidence by scientists, such as Professor Ian Stevenson at the University of Virginia, that reincarnation is a reality. Professor Stevenson studied children from all over the world who remembered their past lives, and confirmed the details contained within them. The book *Children Who Have Lived Before* by Trutz Hardo has detailed accounts of such investigations, revealing through these children's stories that reincarnation is a reality for all of us.

18

Children who see further than most

Know, therefore, that from the greater silence I shall return,
Forget not that I shall come back to you, A little while, a moment
of rest upon the wind, and another woman shall bear me.

Kahlil Gibran

Reincarnation can be defined as a rebirth of the soul in a
new body. His Holiness the Dalai Lama has been reborn
thirteen times. Since the first Dalai Lama, each reincarnation has succeeded in bringing peace and wisdom not only to
Buddhists but to many around the world. But how was the Dalai
Lama found?

Looking for the boy destined for greatness

In order to find the present Dalai Lama, the Regent of Tibet took
a journey to Lake Lhamo Lhatso in southern Tibet. For centuries

the Tibetans had observed that visions of the future could be seen in this lake. Here the Regent saw, among other things, three Tibetan letters, followed by a picture of a monastery with roofs of jade green and gold, and a house with turquoise tiles. The vision contained enough information to seek out the next Dalai Lama.

When finally the high lamas and dignitaries found a place matching the description of the secret vision, a high lama, government official and two servants disguised themselves as traders and found the house that was seen in the vision.

There they found a two-year-old boy, who soon became comfortable with his visitors and he began to play with the rosary which had belonged to the previous Dalai Lama. In a dialect unknown to the district he lived in, the child demanded the rosary, claiming it belonged to him. He later addressed the government official by his proper name and identified the high lama and servants. Astonished, the men left the village only to return with tests to help determine if this child was the Dalai Lama.

In the first test the child was to identify objects that personally belonged to the previous Dalai Lama before him. He was to choose the correct items from carefully crafted duplicates; items included spectacles, a pencil, a bowl and a small hand drum. He passed the test quite easily.

Next, the child was examined for eight distinguishing marks of the Dalai Lama. After finding three of these marks, the examiners were so overcome with joy that their eyes filled with tears. There was no doubt that the two-year-old boy before them was the 14th Dalai Lama of Tibet.

Learning from children

Not everyone's incarnation holds such vital memory reserves as those his Holiness experienced as a child. Did you have an imaginary play friend when you were young? You'd chatter away as you played games or lay in your bed—you even called them by a special name. They were fun to be with. It is a wise parent who does not dismiss a child's ability to see Spirit. Ideally, you could ask questions of your child like: 'Is your friend a boy or a girl?', 'What's their name?' or 'Do they live far away?' All typical questions you'd ask if the friend were a child at school. By showing a general interest and not showing an alarmist attitude, you will allow your child's natural psychic ability to gradually develop rather than suppressing and eventually switching off their intuitive faculties.

Everyone is born with intuition—it is their basic survival right, and if the family can accept this is a natural sense like seeing, hearing and feeling, then the child will feel secure and open to expressing what they sense. Never dismiss a child's warning, 'I don't like that man'. Just maybe they have picked up psychically that 'that man' is not a good soul and they could be in danger. As adults, we can at times override our natural tendencies to 'listen' to our internal prompts and warning bells. Children are pure and not contaminated with opinions and religious dogma that would see them closing off their God-given birth right.

Some will see physical presences around them—they may tell you they have seen Nanny and she told them certain things. Rather than be stressed, try to be open to what they are communicating and why. If they feel they can't openly express to someone what they are witnessing, they may start to feel different, or believe they are weird as no-one else speaks of seeing the same things. Children of this generation have more awareness rising from the media with movies and TV shows such as *The Sixth Sense*, *Medium* and *Ghost Whisperer*, to cartoon characters Scooby Doo and Casper the Friendly Ghost, to remakes of the beloved Peter Pan and Wendy, to the ever-popular Harry Potter—all with shades of spirits, ghosts, angels, fairies and supernatural forces, enough to stimulate lively conversations.

The child who exhibits great sensitivity to criticism and noise, has been laughed at, and has problems with crowded areas could well be the naturally gifted psychic of the family and may need more understanding, tolerance and encouragment to verbally express their feelings. Like what happened to me and many psychic children, life becomes more exciting in the 'real world' and their attention becomes more aligned with worldly fun and needs.

There are the children who from a very young age know exactly what they will be when they grow up—and achieve such dreams—perhaps a stirring from a past life brought forward to completion in this life. Such was the story of a young man called Alexander, who was working in the fields one day. He was the son of a poor Scottish farmer and he heard cries of help coming from a young man who was stuck in a bog, terrified as he was waist-deep and unable to escape. Rushing to help the distressed young man, Alexander was able to cut down a branch from a nearby tree, outstretching this to the young man who was able to grab hold of it, allowing Alexander to pull him to his freedom.

The next day a carriage pulled up in front of his family's farmhouse and a nobleman alighted, introducing himself as the father of the rescued boy. He was so grateful for the gift of his son's life, he wished to offer a reward to Alexander. He asked the young man what he aspired to do when he grew up, and he indicated he would like to be a doctor, but considering their humble background that would never be the case. Alexander's reward for his brave act was his paid education by this man that ultimately saw him graduate from St Mary's Medical School in London—in fact, his name was Alexander Fleming, who discovered penicillin.

Years passed then the nobleman's son became stricken with pneumonia. Rushing to his aid was a young Scottish doctor who administered his wonder drug, penicillin, to this very ill gentleman.

This would be the second time that Alexander Fleming had come to the rescue of Winston Churchill. Yes, it was Winston's father, Randolph Churchill, who had paid for Alexander's medical education that ultimately gave the world the life-saving drug of penicillin. Alexander Fleming had a stirring as a poor farm boy that he wanted to be a doctor—maybe he could see what he was to achieve in this lifetime. A life of the highest calling for mankind. Indeed Spirit manifested, guided and propelled Alexander's soul birth into a family and social background where one day, divine timing would play its hand in connecting him to part of his soul grouping—that of the meeting with Winston and Randolph

Churchill. For Alexander's mission and interaction with his soul grouping had a predestined path that was to see him attend medical school and then on to the discovery of penicillin.

The connection a child has to one particular member of the family, which is often instant at birth—they just clicked with that grandparent, aunt or uncle, considered by some as 'favourites'— in fact could be a recognition, a loving emotional connectedness to that person in their current body, from the child's previous life. Remember, the soul has DNA memory—if the memory of that person is warm, kind and endearing, the bond will be electric, and equally if the attachment was cold and abusive, you may see distance exhibited in this lifetime. A child's phobia or fear that cannot be linked to an incident or event in this lifetime; may well be resurfacing a past soul DNA memory. Children can see further than most, bringing to this lifetime stirrings of their past through memory, gifts and potentials they exhibit. Be open—what you consider imagination may well be fact!

19

Transition of spirit

Souls never die, but always on quitting one
abode pass to another. All things change, nothing
perishes. The soul passes hither and thither, occupying
now this body, now that, passing from body of a beast
into that of a man, and then into a beast's again. As a
wax is stamped with certain figures, then melted, then
stamped anew with others, yet it is always the same
wax, so the soul, being always the same, yet
wears at different times, different forms.

Pythagoras

As a child, I was never satisfied with the stories I heard about God—I would contemplate to myself: 'Who was God's father? Who was his mother? And how did so many people who have died all fit up there in heaven to be with God?' I couldn't see God, yet I was told I had to pray to God, my heavenly father, and that he would hear and answer my prayers, but how could he answer my prayers if I couldn't see him?

I was both confused and curious to understand why there were so many ideas about God—why were there so many different religions and churches if we all believed in one God? My parents insisted I attend Sunday school, and I would come to learn more about God there. It didn't matter which faith, as long as I attended, they said. I must say, I did have a great time as I drifted from one class to another, one denomination to the next.

Always on the side there were the secret visits with my parents to the Spiritualist Church services, where psychic mediums would give proof of the existence of life after death. In the development circles my parents attended, I heard spirits manifesting, giving accurate evidence of their new lives and who was there to meet them when they arrived on the other side. Some had grandparents or family friends welcome them over, even the occasional loving pet found their way to greet them. They were healed of the illness, pain and suffering that they experienced on the earthly plane. They were capable of sending messages filled with love, compassion, hope and encouragement to their loved one with the aid of the psychic medium at the service.

Occasionally, a message was received from a soul had who died at their own hands—suicide. It would appear they had undergone a rapid process of transformation and healing. They had been shown how their actions had affected those they left behind, and although they were allowed to enter the afterlife they would need to attend a 'special school' to understand the consequences and then eventually be sent back to earth to work through their karmic path in another life. Here they would work once again through their blueprint of the soul in the hope of becoming stronger and more confident in this new life's journey, having gained lessons and abilities that would aid them to overcome the obstacles of the past life.

This revelation confused me more—I'd been taught in church that when an individual commits suicide the soul does not go to heaven, and in some faiths they could never be given a church funeral as they were doomed to purgatory. Perhaps this was another story akin to what our history books tell us—that there once existed the notion that the world was flat and if you continued to the edge you would fall into the unknown! Of course, we know now this to be ridiculous. So what does happen when death is upon us? Where do our souls go—do they go anywhere?

The departure

Do we really know what happens to the soul/spirit at the moment of death? There has been much research and many books written over the centuries with hypotheses as to what individuals propose occurs when death finally comes. The great fifteenth century Italian artist Leonardo da Vinci once said: 'While I thought I was learning how to live, I have been learning how to die.'

I sense that at the moment of death, the soul completely detaches itself from the body and the organs, immediately followed by the departure of the vital force. I would suggest it's much like the shedding of all your clothes. I've heard a number of spiritual masters suggest that the soul returns the same way they came to this earth—to the ether, then from the ether to the air and from the air it becomes smoke. From the smoke the soul becomes a mist and from the mist it becomes cloud and from cloud—rain.

It's the moment we are reborn to another life, like the cyclic seasons of Mother Nature, the sparseness of naked trees gives way to glorious foliage when spring is near. From out of darkness does come light. Consider the silkworm—its life is very short, thriving on the mulberry leaves then spinning its golden-threaded cocoon. It's eventually nestled in silence, until just at the right time it emerges to mate, lay eggs, and then die. The legacy is the majestic gold thread prized by so many, and the prospects of a living legacy with new life to spring forth from the eggs laid, contributing to the circle of life.

Every life leaves a legacy, through family, friends and associates. The relationship they shared with those closest will hold lessons usually bound by karmic ties. I don't believe in soul mates— I think it's the biggest con job the media has done to sell books and give people an unrealistic expectation that there's only one person in the entire world who will be the only great love of their life.

A person can be devoted and in love with their partner, only to have that relationship end through death. Down the track they may meet someone else and fall in love once again, besotted with their new love and life. This then becomes a soul connection. Not only will a love interest be a soul connection, you are also connected karmically with parents, friends, work colleagues, your children and next-door neighbours. Remember, life is a school, with many classes and lessons to learn. You will be energetically attracted to those individuals at different times in your life's cycle to experience a transition of your spirit as part of your soul's development, lesson and mission.

Therefore not all souls will experience the same journey or transition of their spirit to the afterlife at the moment of death. For those who die tragically, they will be in a state of shock, disbelief, and some do not see themselves dead. They may hover around the death scene or rush to observe their loved ones until finally they understand they have actually departed from the physical plane. Many souls will hold back from the final crossing over until they are confident that their families have been informed of their passing, as though this is the final act of service to their beloveds. I have known spirits who wanted to be present at their funerals to give comfort to those they loved who were mourning their deaths. Others had already crossed over before the funeral service.

There are mixed schools of thought that say the soul lingers for three days, seven days and some say eleven days before finally making the transition of the spirit to the afterlife. I sense it is very different, depending on the impact and type of death. For those who murdered individuals, their complete crossing over may need the help of a soul retrieval expert; others may need to be enlightened through a psychic medium to understand the errors of their ways, and the impact their deeds had on the life they took.

Many will not be convinced that they are truly deceased and will need assistance to move towards the light. For the vast majority, the transition of the spirit is quick—they're received into the heavenly realms with love and compassion as they take the journey with a loving relative or friend who has come forward to assist in the transformational process. Many relatives speak of their dying beloved talking to someone next to their bed, like in the story of Elaine's aunty in the palliative care unit, and how she saw her deceased sister calling her.

I sense the crossover into the heavenly realms is like a birthday party, a celebration to mark that new 'birth day'—the rebirthing of the soul. Just as in your earthly parties, not everyone could be present due to other responsibilities, so is the case for the spiritual birth day. Some nearest and dearest will have already advanced into other levels of soul development—they may have already reincarnated to earth again. I know many dearly departeds do get the benefit of meeting up with their parents or loved ones—some meetings are brief as their loved ones need to advance onto their soul's mission. Just as you're reading this book at the moment, your family members may be outside playing, at school or at work. It doesn't mean you don't care—they're in your thoughts, but you're participating in a different activity. So is the case on the other side.

Some spirits may need to go to 'healing school' for total restorational purposes, others may need schooling with masters and spiritual teachers to learn more about where they've come from and where they are to go in the future. Yes, learning never ceases—there's always something to benefit, always something to know, something to be shown and something to be completed.

20

Death by destruction

Hold on to what is good even if it is a handful of earth,
Hold on to what it is you believe
even if it is a tree which stands by itself,
Hold on to what you must do even if it is a long way from here,
Hold on to life even when it is easier letting go,
Hold on to my hand even when I have gone away from you.

Unknown

The female voice on the other end of the phone sounded weak, even inaudible at times as she stuttered her words when she spoke. 'I just heard your interview on the radio. You were giving readings to listeners on air and I liked the feedback you received from the callers. I really would like a reading. I'm very sad at the moment—can you see me as soon as possible?'

Fortunately, I did have a gap the following week. To this day, I don't recall her name, only the circumstances of the reading. For ease of reference I'll call her Ruby, and her son Jacob.

Dying for peace

'Welcome Ruby, please come inside—that's your chair over there,'
I said, pointing to a large yellow leather lounge chair. Her small
frame seemed to be lost as she positioned herself comfortably.
Obviously very nervous, her little hands were still shaking as I
explained how I conducted my sessions. 'I will need you to pass
me something that belongs to you, like a ring, watch, car keys or
perhaps a pen. It must belong to you. This is called psychometry,
and by holding and feeling the object I am able to tune into your
vibrations. That's how I do your reading. I don't use tarot cards.'

Ruby gave me her round-faced gold watch and the information followed rapidly. Suddenly I was aware of a male presence
standing behind Ruby's chair.

'Ruby, there's a young man standing behind you—he's rather
tall and lean, with dark hair, with what looks like a priest's collar
around his neck. He's telling me he committed suicide. I see him
standing at the top of a cliff, and he points to the rocks below. I
can see large ocean waves pounding onto the foreshore. He tells
me his depression was so great, he felt lost with no direction. His
pain was too great—he felt he didn't belong, didn't fit into society.
His heartache was unbearable. I sense one of his issues concerned
his sexuality—that he was gay and never had the courage to
acknowledge this to his family or to himself.'

Silently in my mind I asked him if this was the case, and he
nodded. He explained he didn't have the courage to tell his mother,
least anyone else in the family. 'They were so religious, how would

they be able to cope with this as well as my depression?' he said. He felt his only option was to take his life, believing this would release him from the demons that haunted him. True, that day I was the psychic medium bringing the message from a loved one to someone dear, but as a mother, my heart went out to Ruby. With many years of experience in this field, nothing shocks me and I have learnt to be compassionate and non-judgemental. So when I receive revelations and knowledge that would be very confronting to the client, I go 'softly, softly'—my approach is calm, hopefully soothing and gentle, thereby explaining in simple terms what has been revealed by Spirit.

I indicated to Ruby what the gentleman had indicated to me— the confusion that existed around his sexuality. He explained that since his arrival on the other side it had not been 'all beer and skittles'—it's been very hard work. What he thought would be peaceful and a state of bliss in fact had been like going back to school.

'Nan kissed me when I arrived, then turned her back and waved goodbye, saying as she left that I had many lessons to learn while here in the afterlife—I had been a naughty boy! And this time around I would definitely learn the consequences of my actions. Then I was given a flashback to my death and how it greatly affected everyone. Mum, I am just so sorry, I didn't realise the pain I would inflict on you—please forgive me.'

With that, Jacob disappeared. Ruby had lost all the colour in her face.

'Ruby, did you know that young man?'

'No, I don't Georgina. My son was murdered. Here, I'll show you a photo of him.' She pulled out of her bag a rather large portrait taken in black and white, of her son, Jacob.

'Why, Ruby this was the man standing behind you. He was not murdered, he killed himself.'

Ruby burst into tears. 'Oh Georgina, if the church knew that, they would never have given him the burial he deserved. I just didn't want to believe he would take his own life. I didn't want friends and family to think he did that—I was ashamed. Growing up, I remember the church had said if anyone commits suicide it was a mortal sin and those who committed such a sin can't be buried in consecrated ground. I couldn't have that for Jacob, my beautiful son. I feel so guilty, so helpless—I should have done more.

'Yes, you're right, he was depressed. He was on very strong medication from the local general practitioner, but the mood swings were getting greater. He had an appointment to see a psychiatrist the day he died. They discovered his body lying on rocks at the base of a seaside tourist lookout. Georgina—does he have enough clothes to wear? I was so concerned that he'd be cold, as the only clothes he had on were wet when they found his body on the rocks.'

I gently explained that the body we bury or cremate does not have its spirit or the vital force intact. It pulls away like energy from the body to the ether to move towards another realm—some call this heaven, some say the afterlife.

'Ruby, it's very much like shedding your own clothes, the spirit sheds the physical body, so please don't fret about Jacob not having enough clothes. From what I observed of him standing behind you with the priest's collar on, he looked well kept and neat, with his hair combed.'

She seemed relieved, as though the weight of guilt had been taken off her shoulders.

'Ruby, there's one thing I don't understand—what's the significance of the priest's collar?'

'Jacob always wanted to be a missionary, a man of the cloth. It was something he had only shared with me—I guess it was his way of proving he was here today with me. I'm sorry I didn't acknowledge it was him when you first asked me. Just the thought of him actually killing himself—I guess you could say I've been in a state of denial.'

I jotted down some contacts for Ruby to make, to assist her through her grief process, and escorted her to the door. She still had tears in her eyes, and she turned to me and touched my hand.

'Thank you Georgina, I feel a sense of some peace. I don't think I will ever recover from Jacob's tragedy; however, I feel today something clicked inside me. I feel I can now put things in place in my head. Maybe tomorrow I can be more confident and tell the family the truth—thank you again.'

21

Pain of those left behind

In the midst of despair or pain, you may be
convinced that no one has ever felt this way before.
Yet there is no pain you can experience that has not
been experienced before by another in a different time
or place. Our emotional world is universal.

Christina Feldman

Losing a child through suicide presents its own dilemma—it brings to their loved ones a mixture of confusion, guilt, shame and a deep despair. Some believe through their religious or cultural training that their loved ones may be lost in damnation, perhaps to linger in purgatory or hell. Many parents and loved ones hold onto the guilt that they should have known or been aware of the thoughts and actions of their dearly departed. Perhaps then they could have done something to stop the suicide from occurring.

The Mental Illness Fellowship of Australia says that:

> More people—about 2500 people each year—die in Australia
> from suicide than from road accidents. It is estimated that for
> every suicide there are some 30 other attempts. Among young
> people, suicide is second only to road accidents as the leading
> cause of death. Each suicide involves a complex interaction
> of factors, and no single determinant is necessary or sufficient
> for it to occur.

Many of those who take their own lives have been suffering from
a mental illness or a chemical imbalance. In our society there is
enormous pressure to fit in. Many find solace in alcohol and drugs.
For others, what triggers their suicidal intent can be the loss of a
partner, severe conflict in one's life, unemployment, family break-
ups, and for some a history of childhood abuse. For many families
the question will remain—why? Just like Ruby, sometimes the
answer to this question is revealed in a consultation with a psychic
medium.

Ben's answer

Switching on the radio to listen to Kyle and Jackie O, Ben just
caught the start of 'Dearly Departed', and he was taken aback with
the relevance and accuracy of the information being given to the
listener from the deceased. As some listeners do, he became very
emotional—the session was broken with an ad break, and a song

played and tears rolled down his face. He was unable to continue driving, and pulled over to the side of the freeway. He sat in silence as he listened to the words of the Christina Aguilera song 'Beautiful'.

The words spoke to him, bringing great significance and meaning as this was the song played at his ex-girlfriend's funeral a month ago. Ben had been indeed struggling, blaming himself for her suicide. He felt that hearing the 'Dearly Departed' segment followed immediately by the song was a sign. He hadn't known where to turn, where to go, who to talk to, or why he felt so guilty—and maybe I was just the person who had the answers for him.

All I knew when Ben booked the session via email was that he required a Dearly Departed session. Ben was drop-dead gorgeous—tall, with an olive complexion and such a warm, gentle spirit emanating from his soul. My new reading room's colour theme is red—it's grounding and colourful, and often takes many by surprise as they believe all psychics have everything purple! He commented how lively it felt, he liked the colour.

Ben took the seat to the right side of my round table, and I sat to the left. My small table is covered with an assortment of objects that are dear to me—some unusual, beautiful crystals, for energy, that I have collected from all parts of the world on my travels, two red candles in angel candlestick holders and my mum's old crystal ball (only for effect—I don't use it). I asked Ben for the name of the deceased, the age at death and how long they'd been gone—that's all. For me, having this information is like having a telephone number to call someone to have a conversation—

somehow I am able to connect to the other side with these small fragments of information.

'I also have a photo of Natalie, would that help?' Ben asked.

'Sure—I'll place it in front of me,' I replied. She was equally as attractive as the man sitting opposite me. I closed my eyes and said a silent prayer asking that I be able to bring information forward to benefit both parties, Ben and Natalie, when suddenly I started to choke. I remember grabbing my throat, as it was cutting off my air supply—I couldn't breathe.

I have discovered over the years, that for me, the deceased will role-play in my body how they passed. I am not always able to accurately claim how I know the person passed, but in suicides usually the effect is most evident. I could smell a strong odour of alcohol. I then saw a garage and what appeared to be a young woman hanging from the eaves. I remember seeing a teddy bear. Much of the reading I can't recall, as I speak rapidly and do not retain much of what I'm given. I was shown that this young woman suffered from a personality disorder—I felt strongly that she was bipolar, and that it ran in her family, on her father's side. She was a heavy drinker, and she drank to mask her depression. Finally, when the timer went off, I opened my eyes. I had heard Ben sobbing during the session, but powered on. Now I came face to face with his suffering.

Yes, Natalie had committed suicide in the garage, she had been drinking excessively before and she did have the habit of drowning her sorrows in alcohol. The teddy bear Ben had given her as a gift in their courtship, and on the day she killed herself she had placed it on the front door of his house. Ben was feeling responsible for her death—if only he hadn't broken up with her, maybe she'd be alive today.

As we explored the reading, she gave messages, declaring she had been diagnosed a manic depressive, but never told anyone, refusing to take the medication prescribed by her physician and preferring to drink the bad feelings away. There were special messages for her parents, and some personal details for Ben to reflect on and some hope of a new love she was sending for him— a replacement that would give him love and happiness to come. Then I noticed a small smile on his face.

'You know, Georgina, speaking to you I'm starting to realise that Nat did have a problem. I broke off the relationship because of her drinking—I never did realise or understood she drank because she was sad. Everyone knew she was a drama queen. My God! It wasn't my fault, I didn't kill her.'

I could sense a release of healing was starting to wash over Ben—perhaps now he could live with the knowledge that although he may have triggered an emotional episode in Natalie's life, in fact this young woman had a number of mental health issues. As I opened the door to let Ben leave my apartment, he asked, 'Can I give you a hug?'

'I'd love that!' His tall frame leant down and gave me the biggest bear hug—and I knew he would make it.

22

Spiritual school

Why do we fall?
To learn how to pick ourselves up.
Alfred Pennyworth

'Life is a school' so they say, and Jacob soon learnt when he entered the heavenly realms that there was no easy path. All his lives—past, present and to come—were learning fields. What he didn't learn this time he would need to work through in the next life. Heaven is not a laidback holiday resort where harps are being played and you gain your wings on admission—it is a spiritual process, in fact, a spiritual school where you earn the right to move forward as you come to understand the circumstances of your past.

Already, Jacob had been shown his death and how it had affected those nearest and dearest to him, to help him comprehend the impact of his actions on his loved ones. I sense Jacob's entry into the spiritual school system would start with 'healing school', where he would be taught skills by the finest spiritual masters and teachers, gaining insight and revelations about his soul's journey. From there he would graduate into a higher learning field, much like what happens on earth—a tiered school system such as infants, primary, high school, tertiary—and eventually return once again in another form to continue on his karmic path of his soul's development. It may take Jacob years to work through these processes, while others may undergo this phase quite quickly.

What can you do?

When you lose that special person to suicide, hopelessness overwhelms your everyday existence. Your love for them doesn't change—after all love never dies—so open your heart to still continue to send them love. See a mental picture in your mind, or perhaps hold a photo of them as you pray, and they will feel your energies and vibrations—nothing is ever wasted, no thought, deed or prayer. Tell them you forgive them, do not hold grudges or anger—send peaceful thoughts.

You may choose to set aside a quiet time in the morning, evening or weekend, a time when you're not rushed, when you can concentrate and pray for them. You may consider lighting a candle in their honour, as a ritual; a practical way of honouring their life. Forgiveness is divine, and as you work through this process, know that your dearly departed will hear your prayers and receive your love, allowing their healing to move forward, and in doing so they will be happier and more fulfilled in the afterlife.

In the case of murder

I am blessed with a profession that is flexible enough to combine both working opportunities and pleasure activities. So when I was invited to be a guest presenter at London's Mind, Body and Spirit Festival, I jumped at the offer!

Off went the emails to my friends, informing them of my impending trip. The next morning there was an email reply from Alison, my dear friend. 'Georgina, you always stay with me in London when you visit—please come, the apartment is yours! Unfortunately, I'll be in the Middle East on a work assignment, but I'll leave the key with the concierge. You know the drill—just enjoy the trip!'

I quickly responded, thanking her for the generous offer. Alison's apartment is ideally situated within short walking distance of little curio shops, cafes, Kensington Palace, wonderful parks and the underground rail system—it's comforting to go back to familiar places.

I just love how Spirit manipulates circumstances and opportunities to do their will. En route to London I was staying with a former client, now a dear friend, Jules and her husband in Malaysia. In her first reading many years ago, I had predicted how she would meet the man she would marry—and yes, it happened exactly that way. Over dinner one evening, Jules mentioned she was having a girlfriend call around for lunch the next day.

'Georgina, I know you're on holidays and don't do readings, but would you break the rule—just once? Sally has had a lot happening in her life and I'm sure you hold the key to unlock some unanswered questions.'

My friend was gracious enough to open her home, so I agreed. Sally was as entertaining as Jules had described—you wouldn't think for one moment she or her family had suffered quite tragic circumstances—but I soon learnt exactly what those sad events were.

After lunch, we were ushered into the sitting room. 'Sally, Jules mentioned to me you were hoping for a reading while I'm here. Have you got the time now?' I asked.

'Georgina, I have all the time in the world. In fact, I did come prepared—just in case. I have some photos in my bag if you need them,' she said.

I presumed it would be a General/Futuristic Reading. She passed me her watch, and, as always, the words and predictions flowed effortlessly—when suddenly I had the most intense burning, shooting pain in my back, like I have never experienced before. I went into a form of seizure; the pain was incredible, deep within my body. Finally I was able to push away the sensation, compose myself and continue on with the consultation. I went on to describe in detail the vision I saw of a man being murdered—Sally was stunned.

'Georgina, the man you are accurately describing has to be my father. He went missing, and to this day we have never known what happened to him. Yes, there had been rumours as to his disappearance and subsequent death. You have just confirmed for me the reason he left so quickly. In fact, quite some time later a body of a man fitting the description of my father was discovered with knife wounds in his back, just as you described. But this was a number of years ago, when technology didn't exist to investigate further, and also perhaps in our country, murder investigations are not as thorough as in the west. The police couldn't assure us they were the remains of my father. Today you have answered what I needed to know—he is gone, and I can close that chapter behind me. My family will be so grateful.'

23

The cold case

I have come to realise that sometimes my life's work is not where I see it being at that moment. There is a greater plan at work as one meeting or one introduction leads to another—a soul is beckoning to be heard, lessons are waiting to be taught. Closure is needed for new lives to begin.

As I'd promised after the reading, Sally and I caught up for a cup of coffee, and that turned into lunch then dinner.

'Georgina, there's someone close to me who has suffered a similar fate to my family. Someone near and dear to them has been brutally murdered, but there is no resolution. Would you consider helping them?'

The domino effect had set in.

I agreed, although I dislike murder cases because they're so draining. 'Please don't tell me anything about the case,' I asked Sally. 'You know I prefer to operate this way.'

When I opened the door for this client, there stood a very fine-looking man with dark curly hair and a brightly coloured skirt. His voice was mellow and sounded rather English. Immediately upon seeing his face, my heart jumped—I sensed a past karmic connection. We had known each other before—certainly not in this life, but most definitely in a past life.

The first time I became aware of this unusual sensation in my heart was when the doctor rang to confirm I was indeed pregnant with my third child, Brendan. Before falling pregnant, I had a spirit child visit me one evening. He stood by my bed. He looked about two years old, and despite a head full of blond curly locks, he was definitely a boy. He told me, 'You have known me before and I will be returning once again—this time as your child.' As Brendan grew, he developed a head full of blond curly hair—interestingly his two older siblings had dark curly hair at that age.

Obviously, we had had a strong karmic connection from a previous life. In your lifetime you've probably met someone and thought to yourself that you recognised them from a previous association or encounter, only to discover that your paths have never crossed. So when my heart jumps when I meet someone new, for me it is a signal that a possible karmic connection is in front of me.

Mr Charles had a firm handshake, and it rushed through my mind that standing before me was a very well-educated businessman, who had perhaps reached high acclaim in his profession, and that today's consultation would be taking him outside his comfort zone. I believe the eyes are the window to the soul, and I could see the man standing in front of me was indeed an old soul who was deeply hurting. That day he would put aside his education and training and be open to exploring possibilities of a supernatural kind.

I asked that the session be recorded so he could take the information back with him, for further understanding and possible investigation. He passed me a portrait of the woman who had been murdered—Mrs Richards. The events unfolded very quickly in my mind, but her death was played out in slow motion. Suddenly I grabbed my head—the pain was intolerable—it was the blow that killed her. I understand my account was graphic and very detailed—I had seen the murder, I had become the murder victim. I was shown the motives behind the murder and who had taken her life. Rushing before me was the police investigation, interviews and why the case had become 'cold'.

Then, a most beautiful energy appeared and the pace went from rapid to almost feeling like I was floating—the feeling you have when lying back in a swimming pool without a care in the world. Mrs Richards appeared before me smiling, her deep brown eyes showing no hatred or remorse. I became aware of biblical scriptures being quoted and wondered how Mr Charles would handle hearing about this as I sensed he was not of Christian faith. But I have learnt not to edit a session, for what Spirit gives must be for a reason, otherwise they would not deliver this in their messages.

These were beautiful words and heartfelt messages being given from a woman who had been taken so violently from this world. It was obvious she had moved beyond her death to a place of deep healing and looked upon her murder with compassion. Through me she gave suggestions on how Mr Charles could help those she left behind. Then there were the very personal messages that would allow Mr Charles to cut free from the deep state of depression that had engulfed him since her death. How reassuring it is to know that those we dearly love continue in spirit to care for us.

When I opened my eyes, he placed a photo on the table. It was a group photo that included Mrs Richards, and there I saw her killer. I pointed to him. He nodded, and told me this person had been considered a prime suspect. Then he placed another photo on the table, explaining it was the last photo taken of Mrs Richards. I remembered being somewhat surprised, and I think I chuckled, as she was standing in front of a crucifix—it had been taken in church while she was doing the Sunday bible reading.

I looked at Mr Charles, and for the first time he was smiling. He knew that day he had made contact with his special friend. I received a phone call the next day asking if I would care to visit his property out of town. Unfortunately, my schedule was jam-packed—but I did promise to visit when I returned to his country.

The return trip

The plane wheels hit the tarmac, and once again I was back in my favourite Asian city, Kuala Lumpur. The heat hits your face when you leave the airconditioned comfort of the airport lounge. I kept my promise, and was able to meet up with Mr Charles and his partner—this time I would actually holiday at their rural estate and also their villa, with some twenty minutes drive between the two.

My favourite colour is green, and driving through groves of palm trees, coconuts and tropical fruits I felt like I was in heaven—but there was more to this property than Mr Charles was to know.

Years before while living in country New South Wales I had a flash of moving forward in time to a place that was indeed Mr Charles's estate, right down to the fish pond, the wonderful exposed wood beams in the house, to the verandas that gave a 360-degree view of the panoramic hills. The detail was fine-tuned and therefore proof. Yet Mr Charles hadn't even owned the property back then. Looking back now, I can see our past karmic ties were being propelled into the future—once again we would meet in different circumstances to aid the development of our souls' progression.

I had a couple of glorious days. Guests came and went. One night we had retired to sit outside to enjoy the evening breeze and take in the majestic garden that overlooked the valleys, and I had a secret thought to myself. What a mixed group we were—for there were Christians, Hindus, Buddhists, Muslims, a Catholic Archbishop and a psychic! Now where would you ever get that kind of combination?

The days passed quickly and we transferred to the villa—an impressive mansion surrounded with tropical trees and plants. At night-time, the city lights below twinkled from my balcony. With all of its beauty, the energy in the house was overwhelmingly sad. Later I discovered this was where Mrs Richards had been murdered, and residual energy of the event had been trapped in the walls and in the possessions contained in the house. I recommended that to relieve the house of these unwanted energies, they sage or smudge the whole building—this would allow the energies to lift and move on, much like when you have a bath and the dirt is washed away. Sometimes it's necessary to 'clean' the energy in buildings and residences.

On returning home I sent a large parcel of sage sticks to Mr Charles with instructions on how to use them. You simply hold one stick at a time in your hand, light the dried sage and rotate it in a counterclockwise direction, allowing the smoke that emits from the leaves to penetrate the surroundings. I actually love the strong odour of burning sage, and sometimes it's necessary that I sage my own home if I feel a client has brought in a negative presence or when working in haunted or spiritually dark places.

I don't know how my neighbours feel about this strong odour. Several adjoining neighbours have told me, 'We always know when you're awake, Georgina—we can smell the incense. It fills the whole corridor!'

Knowing this and that the smell of sage is rather overpowering, I wait until everyone appears to be asleep before I start my ritual. As I move around the apartment, I send a silent prayer of thanks to the Native American indians for their wisdom of teaching the spiritual qualities of sage and the benefits this has brought to mankind.

Mr Charles's life dramatically changed after his reading—his depression lifted and he excitedly shared with me what he had put in place based on Mrs Richard's message to him. The future looked bright for those whose lives Mr Charles would touch through Mrs Richards's memory and wishes. Although her death was at the hands of destruction, her legacy would be felt through many gener-ations to come—she lives on in the lives she touches. On my first night at Mr Charles's estate Mrs Richards appeared to me—she looked radiant. I could feel her presence in each part of the property—she had found her peace in the world of Spirit, and peace was upon those she loved.

24

Lost souls

In a universe of love there can be no heaven which
tolerates a chamber of horrors.

John A.T. Robinson

The paranormal, ghostly encounters and spiritual presences
have never frightened me—it's like breathing, a basic instinct
of survival of life after death. However, my thoughts changed
a couple of years ago when a national Australian radio show asked
me to be the psychic medium as they conducted a live broadcast
and séance from a well-known jail, said to be one of the most
haunted places in the country. To be totally frank, I thought, 'Here
we go again, another Friday the thirteenth media prank.'

I packed my spiritual protection kit, which contains holy water,
sandalwood oil, a sage smudge stick, matches and coarse rock salt,
and I wore a crucifix and my Spirit of God amethyst pendant for
psychic protection. An amethyst crystal is a superb crystal for
psychically protecting your auric field and warding off evil intent.

As I travelled the two hours up the north coast with Sonja from the radio station, we were talking too much, laughing about the radio stunt, and subsequently lost our way, realising we wouldn't make the 7 p.m. radio broadcast start. Finally arriving at the jail, the transmission was already underway. The magazine I write for had a photographer waiting for some spooky photo opportunities to go alongside the story I was to write about the night's events, so I was rushed into posing in the downstairs cells, lying on wire bed bases, behind bars—anything that would portray the austere living circumstances for the past tenants.

I made one crucial mistake—I didn't apply my sandalwood oil or do my psychic ritual for protecting my aura before going into the jail. Yes, I was wearing my crucifix, which under ordinary circumstances would be enough; but that night I was entering an area known to have residual energy of the darkest kind. Just like a deep-sea diver wears a wet suit for protection against the extreme temperatures, so too I would need additional psychic protective tools to safeguard my own energy field. Leaving the photographer I had just five minutes to walk up the narrow winding iron staircase to the top landing and the commencement of the next floor of cells where I would be interviewed by the radio hosts as to what we could expect that night.

The whole team was so psyched up they were making ghostly noises, jumping out from dark corners, scaring themselves—what a combination of overactive minds! 'Georgina, we need you in this cell. We're going live in one minute. Get your butt in here now,' my radio hosts called out. As soon as I entered the first set of cells, the atmosphere was icy cold compared to just outside the door. Then I felt a presence from behind. Whatever it was held my neck, and I felt intense pain in my buttocks. I doubled up in pain and was overcome with sheer fear and a sense of hopelessness. I started to vomit and choke.

Rushing past the radio crew, looking for an escape, I had to manoeuvre myself down the stairs and find the exit to fresh air as quickly as I could. Even then, I still couldn't throw the ghostly presence away. I knew the only way was to light the large sage stick I had in my protection kit. As the smell of sage circled my body, I felt calmness and clarity and I was once again at peace. The spirit energies had left.

Meanwhile the crew had found the public relations consultant for the jail who subsequently went back to her office to research which tenant had been in that particular cell. The news was bleak. I had entered the death cell of Charles Hines, who was hanged in 1897 for raping his stepdaughter.

I came to realise the vibrations I had tapped into were that of the victim. I had walked into a spiritual hellhole. Hines's residual energy of evil deeds had become entrapped in the cellular structure of the walls, waiting for the next 'victim' to walk into his vibrational field, so he could affix his tentacles of negative energy upon them. The experience brought home to me that no matter how skilled, informed and trained you are in psychic protection, unless you do protect yourself, unhelpful spirits can and will find ways of manipulating energy—like a psychic vampire—to draw attention to themselves.

Some souls never rest, they are always looking for ways of connecting to the physical plane; perhaps seeking acceptance of their past wrongs in order to be set free. Unfortunately, some of these lost souls will never find resolution for their wrongful deeds and continually wander in energy fields disbelieving they're dead. They seek someone who can move them forward towards the light; someone to help them cross over into the afterlife where they can heal and make penance for their wrongful doings. They will eventually return in another life form to understand and learn the consequences of their actions. Fortunately, there exist people in the psychic field who are skilled practitioners in 'soul retrieval', assisting such tormented souls to cross over. This is a specialist field and should not be attempted without skilled knowledge and training, after all you are dealing with the 'dark' side of life.

25

From tragedy to triumph

It's not what happens to you in life; it's what you do
when it happens that makes the difference.

Ken Marslew, Enough is Enough

O ne thing I can guarantee, we will all be subjected to
some form of grief in our lifetime. How then do we deal
with these dark chapters, is there a unique, special way
of pushing through the pain barrier?

My youngest child celebrated his first birthday in 1986, and
amidst the drought and hardship of the land, I felt blessed to see
him move forward into his second year. This is not the case for
others—reality hit home that some lives are cut short when in the
same year a murderer took the life of beauty queen Anita Cobby.

Anita was on her way home after dining with several friends,
alighting from the train at Blacktown in Sydney, when she was
abducted, robbed, raped and brutally murdered. It was a case that
was in the media for years—even after the trial—and was later made
into a book, which I recall reading in one night.

The murderer's childhoods were splashed in front of the public—they had come from abusive, dysfunctional families, they were tormented souls. Many years later, Anita's parents, who were devout Christians, went on to form a support group for victims of crime based on forgiveness and Christian foundations.

Eight years later, Ken Marslew's son Michael was shot in a robbery at the local pizza shop where he worked part-time. I remember tears fell down my face as I watched a television program many years later that showed Ken visiting the correctional centre where his son's murderer was imprisoned. He chose that day to meet the man and openly forgive him for taking the life of his beloved son. It was one of those moments of television I will never forget, both the father and the murderer crying—the emotions were raw.

In Ken's words, taken from his website for Enough is Enough:

The murder of my son in 1994, I saw the way that people were being treated by 'the system'—by that I mean by the legal system, the government, the judiciary and the broader public. I saw a real need for a holistic approach to dealing with the ills of society. Did you know that there are four-and-a-half times more words in the dictionary to describe things negatively than there are positively? *Enough is Enough* is about teaching people that when you change the way you look at the world, the world begins to change. We firmly believe you can change adversity into advantage, bitter into better and conflict into congruency.

History has demonstrated that often through the death of someone famous, there is a chain reaction among the population. The death of Princess Diana brought the British people together—a country united in grief. There was a similar impact on society with the assassinations of Gandhi and Martin Luther King. After the 9/11 terrorism attacks, I noticed that among clients, associates and friends there seemed to be an ongoing wave of internal stocktaking. Where once these people focused on advancement, career escalation and complaining of not having enough, suddenly there existed a realisation—a new vision through the impact of this tragedy. They came to cherish what was truly the most important thing in their lives—the love of family and friends.

I recall a male client of mine, in his mid-forties, seeking a consultation after this event. The knowledge that he had become a work-obsessed executive with little time for his wife and children was burning him up. He realised his children had grown up before his eyes and he didn't even know which were their favourite TV shows and the names of their friends.

His reading confirmed to me that the life changes he was considering would be successful. That evening he called a family conference, resulting in a decision that he would leave his high pressure job and follow his personal dream of developing an internet business from a home office. He would then have time for the things he and the family craved for—time! Several years passed and I heard from an associate that he has never looked back.

I have come to realise through Dearly Departed readings that there appears to be a greater plan in the Spiritual realms. Souls are chosen—or perhaps they have chosen themselves—to be 'sacrificial lambs', to return to this life with a particular mission, a task that will greatly change the structure of how society thinks and acts. Their deaths have in fact been 'gifts' to humankind to instigate greater change—and for this I thank them!

26

Life beyond the physical world

When I consider the hour that will come
In which my spirit will be one with God
It is then that my joy will be complete
It is then that I will see the whole creation
All of its secrets will be revealed to me
And my knowledge will be perfect
The galaxies will be at arm's distance
I will touch the stars with my bare hands
The beauty of every flower, mountain and valley
No longer will be a secret
And every creature will reveal to me
The immense, awe-inspiring world
Created by God's loving hand
And so I stroll on the bottom of the oceans
Ride a comet through a million stars
Or watch a flower grow
I will look in the eyes of other angels
To meet in them the same beatitude
In which my spirit rejoices.

Unknown

I liken Spirit to a mother who tells her children she has eyes in the back of her head. How does she know her children are up to mischief? She's using her well-honed skills of knowing them 'oh so well'.

So too our dearly departeds know us very well. They will line up amazing synchronicities to pass on messages of love and hope and, in some cases, to put to rest unsolved questions concerning their passing. They orchestrate meetings and divine timing when someone or something can be used as a vessel or a tool, a voice to be an instrument from the life beyond to the physical world. Nothing is impossible as far as they're concerned.

I've been told by many clients after the passing of someone close that they've have episodes of lights going on and off by themselves, and even television sets switching on unaided.

We take for granted how frequently we use our telephone, allowing us to keep in touch with significant others. Perhaps it's this same vibrational frequency and carefree attitude that Spirit see as a portal from their world to ours—a magnetic pull, a manipulation of molecules and energy to transport their inner dialogue to the living. Similar to a dog who can hear a whistle inaudible to human hearing yet profoundly clear to the vibrational frequency of the dog's ears, we too can learn to raise our energy vibrations and tap into the world of Spirit communication; the world of the psychic medium.

Given that radio is made up of frequency waves, it seems a natural communication tool that the 'other side' would be drawn to use as a vehicle to 'tune into' to disseminate their messages. We don't see radio frequencies or waves, yet we trust that when we switch on the radio and adjust the dial to our favourite radio station, we will be instantly connected to the world of mass media—music, the latest celebrity gossip, weather forecasts brought to you by a DJ's voice which is propelled down a microphone into frequencies that are played into your radio band. This, I sense, is how Spirit link their connection to the living. All they need is for you to believe, be observant and be open to receiving.

Spirit is practical—they use signs, movies, songs, feelings, smells, sounds, even taste or a memory to get their cryptic messages across. I have learnt not to question what is given, just to say or write it down and allow the natural flow of information to come through. Once you start to analyse what is given, you lose the spontaneity or free flow of information. This is similar to the feeling of being interrupted when you're in the middle of a conversation and you lose your train of thought.

Learning to be calm and relaxed aids the information flow. Having a faith in what I believe coupled with a dash of patience, I have learnt to stay focused. This isn't an easy task when you're working on live television or radio, where you may well be interviewed by a sceptic reporter or a DJ who is hell-bent on keeping his reputation as a shock jock intact by trying to discredit your gift and abilities.

Life is a school and I'm constantly challenged by Spirit to learn, investigate and understand how they wish to use my abilities for the glorification of their lives. It hasn't been easy. In the past I have become unravelled, frazzled and hard on myself, believing

I could have done more to hone my craft. My mother taught me to close my eyes when doing a psychic reading so as not to be distracted by outside influences, but this isn't a good look while working on television, so slowly I've had to retrain myself to work in a different manner. Those closest to me have commented that they know when I'm 'working' as I seem to get a glazed look in my eyes!

One question that's raised continually in the media is: 'How do you know if it really is the voice of Spirit you're hearing, and not just you thinking it or making it up?' Practice, practice, practice. Many years of life experience, lessons and learning to fine-tune your personal receiver set—the human body—and how your receiver interprets the data from the six senses of sight, hearing, touch, smell, taste and intuition, added to experience and maturity, is where your strengths of discrimination between fact, fiction and delivering an accurate interpretation lie.

I have learnt when I experience an inner stillness within my body, an internal strength and 'a peace that passeth all under-standing', I know that what I am interpreting is correct. Some refer to this as a 'knowingness'. I have found that in some instances when I receive a pain in my body, unless I can accurately predict why I am receiving this message for the client or the deceased, it stays with me! When I hit the right interpretation, the pain or discom-fort instantly leaves.

How does a mother know there's something wrong with her child? She senses danger, a disturbance in the child's well-being. How do policemen know they're hunting the right person for the crime? Some say it's a gut reaction, others call it a hunch. Some say 'things just don't add up', 'something doesn't sit right with me' or 'I smell a rat'. These are all small pieces of the psychic puzzle that on a daily basis we take for granted—what our intuition is telling or confirming to us.

Silence is golden. You know how much easier it is to have a telephone conversation when there is little background noise. You can concentrate, listen and enjoy the exchange with more ease. You can allow stillness into your life and let yourself become more accessible to the small messages, symbols or clues your loved ones are trying to communicate to you.

27

A lost soul finds a voice

They may forget what you said, but they will never
forget how you made them feel.

Carl W. Buechner

I know when we're open to communication, wonderful things can happen. So when the radio station solicited for callers to register for on-air 'Dearly Departed' readings and Jessica had been selected from one of the registrations, I wondered what Spirit had in store for her. The production team had rung Jessica and transferred her call to Studio 2, where I was preparing to 'tune in' to the other side. I was given no information except the caller's name.

I asked the name of the person she wanted me to contact and how old they were at the time of passing. She told me it was Trevor. I asked her to try and recall a mental picture or a happy memory of him, and when she felt she had achieved this she was to say his name out loud three times, after which I would I hang up immediately. I would then try to contact Trevor, taking notes of any impressions, thoughts or words I received.

As she said his name, I went icy cold. Atmospheric changes can indicate a spirit is present, but there was to be a double meaning, as I discovered when I explored my reaction with Jessica later. I immediately started receiving messages from the other side. I frantically wrote pages and pages of information.

Time is at a premium, especially on breakfast radio, which has the highest listening audience of any timeslot in the radio day. Therefore I have to keep to key points that will only take several minutes to repeat on air. This is a hard call, as I believe all the points are usually relevant. But I trust Spirit to lead and inspire me to address what will give the caller proof of life after death.

Then I was transferred to Studio 1, where hosts Kyle Sandilands and Jackie O broadcast their breakfast show from a clear glass studio. From the outside, you can observe the workings of the station and their production crew, who are constantly taking calls from listeners wanting to register for the next on-air reading. Some mornings they field up to 500 callers who want their names recorded on the registry for future readings. In fact, this became so popular and time-consuming they eventually set up an email system for registrations as people just couldn't get through the jammed switch.

I never feel comfortable sitting on those tall, movie-star type seats where the celebrities sit for their on-air interviews. I'm always wriggling, trying to get comfortable—I still haven't mastered this after all these years.

'Headphones,' Kyle said to me.

His voice echoed through the headphones, saying 'We're live to air' as he rang Jessica back for her Dearly Departed session. He set the scene, and then I proceeded to tell her and the listeners what I felt from the other side.

Immediately I heard: 'The hills are alive with the sound of music'. I often hear clues in song and movie titles. I felt that Trevor liked bush flowers and wild things and he liked to go walking outdoors. And then I saw the old TV show *Lost in Space*, and I wondered if this person had actually got 'lost in space'. I wasn't quite sure how to interpret this information. Based on the clues given, I thought there had been an investigation into his passing and that he had been lost.

I sensed he had a break to his right leg because I felt a snap in my own right leg as I tapped into his vibration and energy. I saw fresh peas being picked and then snap frozen in the deep-freeze section of the supermarket. I didn't know what the connection was with his passing.

I could sense he was very concerned that some people felt what he did was emotional suicide. I didn't believe he committed suicide, but I sensed that some people thought, 'If I were you I wouldn't have done that because that's a dangerous activity'. I also sensed he was into adrenal surges—doing things a regular person wouldn't do. I received the words, 'Faith brings sorrow, but through separation/death we can still work through energy with family ties.' This was a message strongly directed to his family.

I believed there was no funeral, as I saw a plaque. I heard quite firmly, 'Put the plaque in the clubhouse.' I didn't know if it was his name on the plaque he wanted or what the clubhouse represented.

I also saw very heavy boots, like hiking boots. Because I had heard the *Sound of Music* song, I instantly thought of moutain climbing. I saw a wallet and I saw money coming out of the wallet and I felt Trevor wanted a trust fund or a benefactor situation set up in his memory rather than people mourning his death.

I heard the words, 'Two people will follow in my footsteps.' I knew it didn't mean they'd pass over like he did, I felt he meant two people would search where he had walked, trying to locate him. I sensed it may have already happened, and those people were closely connected to him, either mates or family members. Trevor's family had lost him in the physical sense, but his spirit was very real. The reading was to be a conclusion that he had passed on to the afterlife.

The proof of spirit communication

'Let's go over some things Georgina said and see if it rings true,' Jackie said. 'First of all she heard the words of the song, "The hills are alive with the sound of music". And bushwalking.'

Jessica explained that Trevor had become lost while he was climbing Mount Everest in July.

'Oh my God—that's well done, Georgina!'

While I was listening to Jackie speak with Jessica, I could now see another meaning—Trevor was alive in a past-life situation.

'You were talking about frozen peas and a snapping,' Jackie said. 'So perhaps he broke a bone or something. Is that true Jessica?'

'No-one really knows what happened,' she replied. 'But we assume that he probably broke his leg or something.'

I piped in and said I felt certain he'd broken his right leg due to the sensation I had experienced while communicating with him.

'So you never found him?' Kyle asked.

Jessica explained that there had been ongoing investigations into Trevor's disappearance and he was last seen near Base Camp at Everest.

'It was freezing there, right?' Kyle observed. 'So when Georgina said frozen peas, he's got lost and he's just frozen somewhere! So like Georgina said there's no conclusion—he hasn't been found?'

'Georgina talked about emotional suicide; people very concerned that he was doing this dangerous activity, and that he was an adrenaline junkie. Is that all true, Jessica?' Jackie asked.

'Yes,' Jessica replied. She went on to confirm that there hadn't been a funeral and a trust fund had indeed been set up in his honour.

I was comforted knowing that Trevor was able to have his wishes known for the plaque to be displayed in the clubhouse, as his memorial. Jessica promised she'd ask Trevor's parents if he was associated with a clubhouse.

Kyle loves having the final say. He declared, 'If I was coming through and I was Trevor, I'd be saying, "Find me and thaw me out!"'

I knew Trevor would be happy that finally his family would be at peace, knowing he had passed over.

Jackie wanted feedback from Jessica about how confident she was that I'd contacted Trevor. And I'm happy to say she felt everything was absolutely accurate and she would be passing on Trevor's message to his family.

I love what I do—to see a glimmer of hope come into someone's world; however, for some clients and for myself, a Dearly Departed reading can be emotional. It can leave me overwhelmed and with no energy, as though I've run a 100-kilometre race. These formats are the most energy-zapping, although they're rewarding for the client. For the psychic or medium, it depletes their natural energy flow. I'm told I lose the colour in my face after one of these sessions.

It's essential to protect yourself from uninvited spirits and spirits lingering on. You know what happens when you connect too many electrical appliances to an outlet; appliances can be damaged, the fuse blown, and a black-out can occur. All psychic mediums are aware of 'psychic vampires', spirits who want to plug into the medium's energy field as a portal to deliver a message or access a loved one. They don't realise the implications on the medium, who is drained of all their energy. Mediums need to be constantly grounded and adapt a systematic checklist of their energy fields upon waking and throughout the day, as well as before and after a reading.

28

Mummy I don't blame you

Death is the opening of a more subtle life. In the
flower, it sets free the perfume; in the chrysalis, the
butterfly; in man, the soul.

Juliette Adam

I wasn't prepared for what Spirit had in store for my diary on one
particular week. Normally I'm booked out for six months in
advance with a waiting list of clients eager to drop what they're
doing if they're fortunate enough to secure a last-minute cancellation. The internet has been a marvellous tool for teaching—having
my own web page, www.georginawalker.com, where individuals can
listen to some of the segments from the radio program, has given
the outside world an opportunity to experience first-hand the
emotion of a connection with someone who has passed over. Many
bookings for readings are done through the email system.

One such enquiry came from Sharon Howard, who has given
me permission to recount her experience. She indicated she was
going overseas later in the week and was keen to have a reading

before she left. Replying immediately to her request, I let her know that I was fully booked and then I deleted her email. Within minutes a cancellation came through, and no-one on the cancellation list wanted that particular time. It surprised me that so many people declined as places are usually snapped up with a phone call or two. Luckily I still had Sharon's email address in my delete folder, and I offered the session to her. It was to take place several days later.

As the elevator door opened, there stood a petite blonde lady who looked quite nervous. She had a strong English accent, and told me that she was heading back to England after a holiday in Australia. The people she was staying with had told her of my radio segment 'Dearly Departed'.

In these sessions I like to focus only on one person who has passed over for the full half-hour. I ask clients to bring an item that belonged to the deceased—a piece of jewellery, a garment they wore or a lock of hair. This gives me an instant connection to their energy imprinted on the item. Some choose to bring a photo; others have nothing but their name to give me. Ultimately, the choice is theirs as to what they provide.

Sharon had two photos in her hand, and I asked her for one of them. She was reluctant to choose, and gingerly handed over one photo. Spirit immediately indicated to me that both individuals in the photos had died at the same time. Normally I don't ask questions in the first fifteen minutes of the taped session. However, I felt I had to ask, 'Did both die at the same time?' Her reply was 'Yes', so I asked for the second photo as well.

Usually, I write down on a piece of paper the name of the person or persons who have passed over, place my hand on the special items brought in, and ask the client to close their eyes and think of a happy memory of the loved one. It could be a scene, a memory or a photo, and once they have a sense of or can see in their mind's eye a memory, they are to say the name of their special person out loud three times.

The benefit of using this technique sees the client becoming more relaxed as they focus on positive memories of their beloved, which in turn reduces the amount of negativity and tension they may have brought into the reading room. This is the same set-up as the one we use on the radio segment. They can then open their eyes and I will start the consultation.

I record each consultation because I speak rapidly and it's hard to take everything in at once. Sometimes clients need to go back over and over the recorded session in the comfort of their own home, and sometimes research is needed on some of the messages and information given, as they may not be aware of facts and information presented. For some, the proof of life after death may well have been signs and details from before they were born.

This was not the case for Sharon, as the two individuals, I was to find out later, were her two sons, Taylor and Mason.

As I held my hand over the photos of the two young male children, I immediately saw a plane trip and a beach resort. I could see a man standing on the beach with two small boys. I could then see a child by a swimming pool. I could feel pain in one of my shoulders, as though I had had an injury to the side of my shoulder and neck. Then I remember seeing a child going to the Spirit world and an older woman in Spirit had come to take him over and was trying to entice him to go with her. She held a bag of boiled sweets—as though she felt this would encourage him to leave with her. There was a cheekiness about him. He said he would go if she gave him popcorn and lemonade. Later Sharon indicated she knew which of her boys this would have been, as that's something he'd have done.

One son indicated he wasn't going without 'Da'. He wanted 'Da' to be with him. Then an old man appeared, and with the most loving, kind and sympathetic words he said to Sharon, as best I can recall, 'Oh Pet, oh Pet'. Usually I can distance myself from emotional involvement in readings, much like a counsellor or psychologist; however, the emotion of this reading was so overwhelming I just burst into tears. One of the children wanted Sharon to know there was no blame for his mummy picking the holiday destination.

Sharon explained that she had chosen Phuket for a holiday with her sons Taylor and Mason, and 'Da' was David, her fiancé, who had proposed to her the night before. One boy was in the child-minding area of the resort; the other was by the pool; and she and David were in their hotel room—when the tsunami hit Thailand. All three were drowned. She lost consciousness and was saved by an Australian; the same person she had come to thank on this holiday in Australia. She believes it was her grandmother who collected the boys. The message from the old man was from her father, who died a week after the tragedy.

As a medium I can't take away the pain, but I trust that I can ease the pain and bring some form of resolution to the mourning process. Sharon pulled a photo out of her wallet. It was the scene I was shown from Spirit of a man with two boys. It was the last photo she had of her three men. She had returned to her hotel room several weeks later to salvage what she could, and had found the undeveloped roll of film that contained this photo. Amazingly, this was the scene so strongly held in my head—yes, Spirit knew about the photo and was letting her know they knew as well.

Although lost in the physical sense, they are with us with every breath we take. Proof is there for the living.

29

Visiting a psychic

If aught I have said is truth, that truth shall reveal
itself in a clearer voice, and in words more kin
to your thoughts.

Kahlil Gibran

'If only I had your gift!' I'm often told by clients. Some may seek
out the ability in order to assist others; however, I would suspect
many wish for a power that will enable them to intuit winning
Lotto numbers, be deemed with a supernatural knowledge that
will shortcut their quest in seeking out their soul mate, know what
the boss is thinking or what's under the Christmas tree. Perhaps
they're looking for fame and fortune!

Every soul is precious, and the prediction of a new soul coming
to a childless couple had one client in a head spin. Sandra, in her
late thirties, arrived for her reading totally emotionally and physically exhausted after six failed IVF attempts. Adoption now seemed
her only option, but Spirit told me she would fall pregnant naturally
and give birth to a baby girl within fifteen months.

'Fat chance of that happening, Georgina,' were Sandra's final words as she left my apartment. The following Christmas, eighteen months later, I received a cheeky Christmas card from Sandra, Paul and their beautiful baby daughter, Bree, who arrived just as predicted!

I've been fortunate to holiday in palaces and be given the title 'Royal Psychic', I've met and read for some of Hollywood's A-list and flown around the world to give one-off consultations to amazing high-profile people. I've been blessed with the opportunity to read for all streams of society, whether it be face to face in my home, through my column or on radio or television. But the road of 'apprentice to Spirit' has been extremely tough.

I recall when Brendan was six weeks old, I was travelling on a rough dirt road when I had a flat tyre. The bolts wouldn't budge. I had no option but to walk with the baby in my arms, seeking help. The farm to the left had a two-kilometre walk to the homestead, while the property to the right was three kilometres ahead, then a further two kilometres inland to the workman's shed. I chose the easier option, or so I thought. Yet I heard in my head, 'Take the far property, no-one is at home here'. I didn't listen.

I must have walked nine kilometres that day carrying the baby in the heat of the midday sun, until I reached the second farm and help. I made a vow that day to Spirit that I would always listen and obey.

My decision to 'blow the whistle' on corruption in my workplace brought rapid decline in my health, loss of a regular income and even the loss of the roof over my head and my beloved dogs. There has always been a test. It's as though I'm spiritually put through a fire, and if I succeed in learning the lesson a new window of soul development is opened, followed by another lesson, refining my nature, my personality, and testing my integrity, honour and goodness.

It's been asked of me a number of times, 'If you're such a gifted psychic, why didn't you know that was going to happen in your life?' Well, sometimes we're not permitted to know the future as it's part of our life's journey, part of the development and extension of the soul's blueprint of life. You can't eat an elephant in one bite, so too a psychic doesn't have access to all aspects of their life or the person they're reading. Some things we need to experience in order to take us to the next step of our life's purpose.

Looking back over my life's progress to date, I can see the wisdom of the universe. Why I was placed in certain circumstances, the downsides and what I gained from that experience. Being deserted and left to raise three children in a single-parent home saw loneliness, stress and hardships, but I also discovered strengths and reserves I didn't know existed within my being. The need for material wealth no longer drove me. When you lose almost everything, you define what you really need and what you can live without.

Love of family became my priority. My psychic ability rapidly developed as I drew more on my inner skills and intuition for survival. I learnt much about human nature and the need to forgive, forget and move on; attitudes and skills I use now when I work with my clients. Would I choose to walk that path again if

I knew what was in store? I remember saying to my mother, 'Why do I have to suffer so much when I believe in goodness and God?'

She responded, 'That's when God can do His greatest work.'

From the vantage point where I sit today, I would have to say yes—I can now see the unique wisdom behind the lessons.

These difficult lessons have refined my inner being. I can empathise with a client because I have travelled down that road or a similar one. I've learnt humbleness—dropped the ego to be just myself. I've had no need for a mask to help me step up a peg in any social setting. I've learnt if people don't like me for who I am, what I say or what I stand for, I won't be invited again, and that's part of my journey.

So what appears to others as a gift can be a curse at times. I don't believe I know any well-developed psychic who has not suffered in some realm of their lives! Not that we want to choose suffering as part of bargaining with Spirit for a gift. I sense the suffering strips the ego bare, and that's when Spirit can do their greatest work, one of building a unique vessel for the greater good of all humankind.

Choosing a psychic medium or intuitive

Think about how you chose your doctor, dentist or hairdresser. For some, it may have been a random event, leafing through the phone book, or through an advertisement in the media or a recommendation. A professional psychic medium is just that—a 'professional'—so you should be discerning when selecting any service for yourself, and use the same benchmark when selecting an intuitive or psychic medium as you do for any professional. Not all hairdressers are good at cutting, perming or colouring hair, and some you would never go back to. The same is to be said in this field.

Consider what you are seeking from that psychic. Some psychics specialise in past lives, others can predict the future, and some are especially skilful in speaking with those who have passed over. Not all psychics are mediums. Mediums specialise in the ability to serve as an instrument that allows communication with those in the afterlife. What tools do they use to access their knowledge? Tarot cards, tea leaves, psychometry, numerology, astrology, photos or trance?

So if it's the future you're seeking, you may well spend your money on someone who specialises in that field. Don't assume, however, that because your friend received a message from her deceased Aunty Flo during a tarot card reading that you will have a similar experience. That may well have been a random act from Spirit, because the reader may have been more open to Spirit communication than on other days.

I have two different formats for readings. One as a psychic medium, for the client who is seeking a Dearly Departed connection to a loved one who has passed over, and the other is a General/Futuristic reading. I no longer offer both formats of readings to one client on the same day. I prefer my client to digest the wisdom and advice given from one sitting at a time. Then they are free to return on another occasion to have the alternate reading.

Word of mouth from a friend or associate will often point you in the right direction when seeking a psychic or medium. One who delivers consistency in their predictions, accessing factual, relevant proof of information from your deceased loved one, gives credibility to their craft.

What kind of reading are you after?

A point of caution here—personalities of the psychic and client can give different expectations and outcomes of the session. Not everyone likes my straight-shooting way of delivering messages. I have a reputation of saying it how it is. So if your style of receiving information is 'softly, softly', perhaps you should seek out someone whose delivery will better suit this.

Does the psychic have a code of ethics, such as confidentiality? Will they tell you the truth? Or do they tell you what you want to hear, so you leave feeling like you're walking on air, but with a false sense of security? Listening to a friend's account of a psychic session, I sensed that the psychic told them what they wanted to hear, not what they should hear. There's a big lesson in this. So think carefully and clearly about what it is that you're seeking— entertainment, or truth and accuracy?

For example, I had a new client come for a reading and I asked how she heard about me—it was a referral from a friend.

My response was, 'They must have been happy with their reading.'

'Actually, no. She hates you. But when I listened to her reading, you told her the truth, which I knew to be the case, but she just didn't want to see what you were saying was correct. That's what I liked about your reading.'

The dissatisfied client surfaced again several years later for another session—the predictions had become a reality. That's why I insist that readings be recorded. People will only take in what they want to hear at the time—not what they should hear. Perhaps they need to reflect when the time is right or when they are prepared to understand the messages given.

You should never be asked to do something that you feel uncomfortable about. I once had a very distressed young girl ring me. She had been to see a male psychic who asked her to lie on a table in her underwear while he did some energy work on her. He even felt her breasts. Another was told to masturbate on a blue carpet and then bring the carpet back to him. There are definitely people who prey on individuals. All professions will have people who do not represent ethical and safe conditions. Walk out, rather than be subjected to dangerous practices.

Getting the most out of a session

Give the psychic minimal information. Allow them to do all the talking and predicting rather than feeding them with information that will impact on what they tell you. A skilled practitioner can assess a client by their body language.

For a General/Futuristic reading, I hold in my hands a piece of jewellery, a photo or an item belonging to the client. I give an introduction on how I do my readings, explaining how I see, hear, feel, taste, smell and talk rapidly as I assimilate and interpret the data that Spirit gives. I actually have a timer that goes off halfway through the session—as time flies—and this allows the client and me to know how we have paced the reading.

At this stage I will wind down, open my eyes and ask the client whether they have any questions concerning the reading. Before clients come to the session I suggest they write down any questions they'd like to ask during the session—for the simple reason that minds can go blank at this stage! Many people say I usually answer what they want to know, but be prepared—it's your time and your investment.

At this point the client can also show me photos of individuals they may have brought to the consultation and ask questions about them. These can be photocopies or originals, as long as there is only one individual per photo. Group photos can be tricky because energies can jump around and I can be focusing on the subject but picking up vibrations from another person in the photo.

Once, a father brought in photos of two young men. In the first one I sensed a scar on a particular part of his leg. When he produced the next photo, the father told me this was the man who had the scar on the leg. In fact they were identical twins—hard call! However, the father could place the message for that individual as accurate.

Naturally, if you are visiting a numerologist or astrologer, you'll need to give dates and names; they need these as tools of their trade that allow them to work with their forecasts.

A word of caution about telephone psychics and mediums— no doubt there are many wonderfully gifted people who work for these services, yet I've had several clients who amassed $8000 to $12 000 in telephone bills with these psychics. If you must use these services, have your questions on hand, decide how much you're prepared to spend for this consultation and set a timer so there are no shocks when the phone bill arrives.

The advantage of booking in to have a face-to-face reading is that if the crisis disappears you can always cancel. Having the telephone so close can be a bit like talking to a friend. Many phone psychics are paid good bonuses to keep clients talking on the phone for a long time. Ask yourself: 'Is this essential? Am I lonely and using this to fill the void? Do I need to speak to a counsellor, priest or someone else about my grief over losing my dearly departed?'

With all consultations, don't feed the psychic too much infor- mation about what's happening in your life. Mind you, don't go in there hell-bent on not saying anything. The more relaxed and open you are in thought and physical presence, the easier it will be for the psychic to use their gifts.

Some clients come in for a session so tense and stressed out that their aura or energy field becomes dull, almost fuzzy, because the energy needed to expand an aura is contracted and shattered through their negativity. You know what it's like to drive in a fog—

you have to really concentrate on your driving, slow down, and the journey often takes longer due to the restrictions placed on your visibility. That's what it's like for the psychic medium when clients present in this state. I've never been unable to read anyone, but I have found that with some people I really need to work hard and use far more psychic energy to produce the reading, leaving me by the end of the session feeling as though I've done several sessions.

I have concerns when I hear that a psychic or medium won't allow a session to be recorded. Having a record will allow the individual to have a reminder of the session to work through forecasts and investigate facts. It doesn't mean you should play the tape or CD every day and make the predictions happen. Much like using a road map to get to a destination, you make choices on which route or road you will take. Some take longer, on others you may get lost and are late, but ultimately you reach your destination.

So too a reading can give you warnings, detours, stops and starts, and confirmation of a direction. It is up to you to make these choices—you were given a brain and a free will to make choices in your life. If someone told you to put your head in the oven, you wouldn't; so too be aware of false prophets—psychics who give unstable advice. There are people in this field who operate on the dark side rather than work in the light of goodness, wholesomeness and rightful ways.

Not all psychics deliver their information in the same package. I can get names, letters, dates and messages from the other side in a General/Futuristic reading. Each reading is individual and varies from one consultation to the next. Spirit has the say in what is to come through. I'm the vessel that receives, and then I interpret the information; just like a television is non-operational until connected to electricity and switched on to a particular channel for viewing. Sometimes there can be technical difficulties and the screen goes blank.

Sometimes the reception isn't clear and needs to be fine-tuned. The psychic or medium's level of maturity, experience, practice and life skills have enormous impact on processing the data and giving interpretations. There are some brilliant psychics who deliver information in different formats. Don't discard a psychic because they can't give you all the information you may be seeking. Consider that maybe Spirit doesn't want you to have this information at this time. Maybe they have delivered a health warning that's far more relevant to your circumstances than what you came for. You can't make a psychic give what they can't get.

Timing can be more fluid

Don't discard your recorded session if none of the consultation rings true—perhaps the events and information given on that day are to come, and you may not be able to relate to some of the predictions made until a later date. I had one lady contact me saying that after seventeen years a prediction had come true. She lived in outback Australia when I gave her the reading, telling her she would move to a coastal area and would work in the sugarcane industry. At that time in her life she thought the scenario to be impossible. However, seventeen years later, she moved states and worked in that industry.

Remember, Spirit doesn't have a clock—it's us humans who have developed the concept of time. That's why so many people find that when a psychic gives a time frame, it may not eventuate precisely. Once I told a woman I could see the number five, and that she would be retrenched from her job. I felt that it was to be quite soon, perhaps five months. She rang me the following week and said, 'Thanks Georgina, it was five days.' I had the numeral from Spirit, but, humanly, I went with months. So now I always use this example to clients to help them understand timing and numerals, to assist them with their expectations of a reading.

Be aware of opposites

Ask the psychic if they see in black and white or in colour. 'Negatives', used in film photography, when held up to the light show an opposite image to the positive one that will appear when the film is processed. For example, a black and white negative will show a dark-haired person as fair-haired—reverse imaging. Some psychics actually see things like this. Also, numbers can be seen as mirror images; for example, if I see a 67, I make sure I tell the client that it may also be a 76.

If I'm working in clairsentient, or clear feeling mode, and receive a pain in a particular part of my body, it could well be the opposite side for the client. Perhaps we psychics are somewhat dyslexic in how we read and experience our senses.

Psychic mediums work in different parameters as well. Some see Spirit as a solid form standing next to the subject; they can feel its presence and hear what it says. Others 'tune in' to the other side. I can see physical form, hear and feel its presence. Just like you need a number when dialling the telephone, I find having a 'tool' such as a photo, age at time of death or something of the loved one to hold makes the connection quicker. A wonderful aspect of working in this area is that sometimes Spirit arrive in my home before their earthly loved one arrives for the consultation. What a bonus that is—they are obviously excited and are looking forward to the connection.

30

Talking to the other side

I am like a falling star who has finally found her place
next to another in a lovely constellation where we will
sparkle in the heavens forever.

Amy Tan

Conversing with the other side is not like having a conversation with your best friend. It's energetically draining for both parties. So for me Spirit use a code, giving information in songs, movies etc., and the client may need to research the message. They will hold up a flash card with a name or initial on it. Many believe their beloved will come through as angelic, happy and fun loving. Personalities don't change once loved one go over to the other side, and if they were cranky and sharp, their personality will be the same in the delivery of a message. They can be critical, loving, humorous, but above all they wish to connect.

Do your homework

Sometimes clients need to do homework regarding information given at a session. Spirit can divulge facts from a time when the client was young, perhaps even before they were born and so they would not hold a memory. I always get excited when I receive an email or a letter from a client joyously confirming details, names or events given by their loved one. I recall one client came bringing a lock of hair from her infant child who died in utero. I kept hearing Spirit say, 'He looks just like a China doll.' Later the client told me the child's father was Asian, and her son would indeed have looked like a little Chinese doll. It was such a wonderful relief for her to see Spirit acknowledge this baby's soul.

Another woman brought a wristband belonging to her deceased child. Immediately an older gentleman in Spirit came through with the child, telling me his name was Charles. She couldn't place the name. That night I received an email saying her husband's grandfather was Carlos, and Charles had been the English name given to him. She told me how she and her husband cried with tears of joy knowing that their child was with family on the other side. Just as Carlos used the English version of his name, sometimes the departed who had minimal English conversational skills when they were alive are still able to impart a dramatic message with quite detailed information to their loved ones.

You will need much patience in your search for communication from your loved ones. As I have mentioned, different mediums have differing strengths and weaknesses and so do those dearly departed souls in the Spirit world. Some days they will be chatty, while others they may be quiet. You must have had a conversation with a relative or friend that was hard-going because they just didn't feel like talking. It's the same in the heavenly realms; personalities don't change just because they have passed on. Your beloved may be busy overseeing another family member or working on a divine plan and not in the mood to be interrupted.

Children often come through very excited to catch up with their mum and dad, letting them know they had no pain making the transition and have met up with their grandparents and even some pets. Yet their actions and symbols are often far more impressive than their level of conversation. You won't find a five-year-old child speaking with the same level of conversational skills as a 30-year-old adult. It may take several visits to a medium over a period of time to allow confidence, rapport and energy to build up to successfully get a total picture of what they wish to communicate with you. This is why it is essential that no matter who you see for a consultation, keep all your notes and recordings.

Tony drowned in the family's swimming pool when he was four years old. Their pet labrador, Charlie, had alerted the family with his barking, but it was too late. His mum, Pru, found him at the bottom of the pool. On the second anniversary of Tony's passing, she decided to have a reading. Tony came through immediately; he was holding a beach towel and a kick board in his hand, jumping up and down with excitement. Pru found this very distressing, why would he be so excited to go swimming when he died in a pool?

When I described the colours in the towel and the markings on the board, Pru covered her mouth in shock. 'Georgina, we had bought those for Tony for Christmas, but he died two weeks before. The presents are still in his bedroom.' Tony held up a painting. He pointed: 'Mummy, Daddy, Chacha and Baby.' Tony knew that he now had a little sister, Katie, who was just three months old. 'Chacha' was the name he called his dog Charlie.

Pru was comforted to know that Tony was indeed watching over them. When Katie was two, Pru decided she was ready for another session. I could sense Tony's presence prior to her arrival. He was very vocal this time, chatting about the new baby boy and that he wanted him to have his bike and cars. He didn't want the baby to have his name; he should be called Toby. Pru was as confused as I was, it didn't make sense. Six months later Pru rang to say she had just given birth to a baby boy who she named Toby. She didn't know at the time of the reading that she was pregnant, but Tony knew.

Some clients have very unrealistic expectations—sadly, there can be no guarantee that you can tap into a loved one. So if a psychic medium guarantees they can contact your loved one, a warning light should be flashing bright and red. Take this as a warning. A genuine psychic will tell you nothing is 100 per cent guaranteed from the Spirit world.

Some mediums will be able to distinguish how the person died, and may give you names of those they are with in Spirit; others may not. Many will be able to tell you about your loved one's person-ality, likes, dislikes, pastimes and interests. It may seem trivial or inconsequential to you; nevertheless it is important to them. Sometimes a person who you least expect will come through and give you a message, not the beloved who you were seeking. I understand this is frustrating for the client and also for the psychic medium, but there is nothing predictable about the afterlife.

31

Psychic protection

The function of wisdom is to discriminate between
good and evil.
Cicero

Have you ever felt totally drained when you hang up the phone after talking to a friend, leaving you with a headache or completely depleted of energy? Have you walked into a shop and felt suddenly spaced out, only to find the sensation leaves when you walk out the door? Or do you feel nauseous or overwhelmingly tired when a certain family member visits? If so, what you experienced was 'energy zapping'. People store negative, stagnant and polluted energy in their bodies, and unfortunately this remains with them until they drop off the energy onto someone else.

My client Frank was worried about his son Sebastian. Whenever Sebastian returned home from visiting a particular group of friends and walked past him, Frank became dizzy and drained of all energy. My guides told me Sebastian was experimenting with drugs which altered his energy field. His aura was leaking energy. Just like a creeping vine seeks out a stable object to latch onto to thrive, Sebastian's leaking energy field was unconsciously reaching out to Frank's powerhouse of energy, depleting his reserves and dumping negative energy on him. Frank needed to learn psychic protection.

Psychically protecting your aura and energies is essential on a daily basis. Prior to visiting a psychic or medium, imagine yourself surrounded in the most beautiful gold light. A qigong master once told me to symbolically paint my aura—the energy field surrounding the body from the top of the head to the souls of the feet—ten times with gold light. I imagine I'm in an eggshell and I see myself being dipped in beautiful gold paint ten times. I find this technique much quicker and more effective. Remember to redo the processes when you've left the session.

Before a client arrives for a Dearly Departed reading, I set aside quiet time where I meditate and pray that I will be used as a divine instrument to assist the client who is arriving for their session, and that the right information will be given for them that day. It is often at this time that the dearly departed will appear, as though they too are preparing for the session and are keen to have this opportunity to express through a medium what they have not been able to say since they passed over.

The way you approach a reading, and allow your loved one to communicate in general, is affected by your outlook and reactions. It is only natural through grief that you may become obsessed in wanting to visit numerous mediums for proof and comfort of your loved one's existence and presence. Consider how your beloved would cope with the continual interruption to their development on the other side. They too need time to refresh, adjust, catch up and learn where they've been and what will be expected for their soul's development in the future.

The afterlife is a continuum of our earthly existence. Your beloved may be found in a 'spirit hospital', enjoying divine healing. Then there are the reunions with loved ones already passed on—kindred spirits embrace those nearest and dearest, excited at the opportunity to meet up once more. Some eager souls enjoy the opportunity of learning from the great masters; while others keen to reincarnate are prepared to enter a stage of learning much like returning to school. There are moments of restfulness and times of great activity in the afterlife. You need to seek balance, both for the living and for the departed.

I find it easier to tap into the energy of the dearly departed when I have a name, or an item that belongs to the individual. Many times in a General/Futuristic reading, Spirit manifests and cuts right through the predictive part of the reading to grab my attention to pass on a message for the client. I am a mental medium. I see things that pop into my head, feel pain or sensations in my body, and hear words, songs and inspirational notes. It's like going over your favourite song—you don't actually hear the words, but you sense them.

There are some psychics whose strengths lie in clairaudience, or clear hearing. The famous English medium Doris Stokes was such a person. Her gift materialised through her hearing ability.

There are a small minority of exceptionally gifted mediums whose facial expressions and voices change as they deliver their messages. A female medium may sound masculine and take on the physical attributes of male energy.

The many great spiritual masters we have had through the centuries possessed wonderful qualities of mediumship and the ability to alter their physical state or produce manifestational changes through their knowledge of matter. Jesus was able to multiply bread and fish to feed the masses; he could walk on water and change water into wine. This concept may shock and insult your personal concepts of biblical writings, yet you are investigating the afterlife. Jesus is a brilliant example of a messenger from God! He appeared to his disciples three days after his passing. He was a great healer, medium and man of the times. Is his legacy one of teaching through example?

This is very controversial, I know; however, if we are to align our thoughts with the fact that there is an afterlife and we leave our physical case, the human body, with the soul leaving to venture to heaven, or the afterlife, isn't that what the Bible says happened to Jesus when he died?

I have witnessed my qigong master, Zhao, stand on raw eggs in their shells. The eggs were cracked open afterwards and poured into a container as proof of what he had accomplished. A manipulation of his energy was needed through much training and discipline to accomplish such a task. So too, Saint Germain, reputed to be one of the greatest alchemists of our times, knew of this secret. Likewise the Indian master, Sai Baba, produced in his hands the ashen-like substance, verbuti. Of course, there are sceptics who say magic and sleight of hand delivers these results and that there is no such thing as people being able to communicate with the dead. So where does that leave Jesus' appearance after the third day? If we are taught to pray to a God or deity that we can't see, yet believe our prayers and requests will be heard and many will be answered, then why can't we believe that through the correct channels we will be able to access the afterlife?

Psychic protection techniques

Just as there is light, so there is dark. If we didn't have the darkness, we wouldn't strive to be closer to Godliness. You need to be mindful that we do not wish to attract Spirit visitations where there are lower frequency individuals—spirits who, when they lived on the earth plane, were deceptive to down right evil—who will try and jump in where, literally, angels fear to tread, influence your daily tasks, mimic people you know and lead you off in wrongful directions. Just as hygiene should be part of your daily ritual, now you need to incorporate psychic protection into your daily routine.

There are books written specifically for psychic protection techniques, with extensive information and workings, so I will just explain what works best for me on a daily and weekly basis. Not all of these techniques will be applicable for you. Just as a person who has false teeth will use a different cleaning method to a person who has natural teeth, the end result will still be clean teeth. The same is true with psychic protection.

Working through from morning to sleep, these are a few solutions and approaches you may like to try.

Aromatherapy, sandalwood oil

I recommend one that has minimal or no chemical residues. Place a small drop at the back of each ankle, inside the pulse point of both wrists, at the nape of the neck, the top of the crown of the head in the hair and on the third eye position, the space between the eyebrows. Be careful not to get this in your eyes as it can sting. This creates a psychic protection circuit around your body. It's similar to applying fabric protection to your new lounge, the stains won't soak in. This will discourage negative energy to seep into your energy field. It can be reapplied during the day.

Crystal protection

Amethyst is the crystal of tranquil dreaming. It symbolises intuition and is a natural choice for psychic opening and intuitive work. Its high frequencies act as a barrier against lower energies, making it a protective tool against psychic or spiritual attack. It activates the higher mind, allowing one to gain a clearer comprehension and understanding of the dynamics and root causes of life experiences. It is crucial, prior to using any crystal, to wash the stone under cold running water to cleanse any negative energy.

Wear amethyst as a pendant or on a charm bracelet, or for babies and young children, hang it as a mobile over their crib or bed for protection and as an aid for sweet dreams.You can also place an amethyst crystal next to your bed for protection. It's essential that amethyst jewellery is unhampered by a solid backing, allowing the stone to convey to the wearer its full energies as it nestles against the skin. All these attributes can be found in my signature jewellery piece, Spirit of God.

In this piece, the perfect equilateral triangle symbolises Mind, Body and Spirit or the Trinity and is housed inside a circle, representing God—no beginning, no end—encompassing the whole person, the whole of humanity, the whole Cosmos. Within the circle lies a bezel-set facetted Brazilian amethyst gemstone. Amethyst engenders communion and communication with one's guides and angels. See www.georginawalker.com.

Gold light technique

Imagine you're surrounded by gold light, from the top of your head to the souls of your feet. This allows protection of your aura—the energy field that surrounds your being. Many psychics recommend surrounding yourself with white light, especially when in a situation of fear, but remember the lower frequencies or dark forces are attracted to the light or white. Purple or blue would be favoured in these circumstances of fear. The gold light can be used multiple times during the day to refresh or protect your energy field.

Salt

You know how good you feel after a dip in the ocean? The salt purifies and takes away negative energy, making you feel alive and refreshed. If this is unavailable to you, a good substitute is rubbing a salt scrub over your body under the shower or in the bath, placing a cup of salt in your bath, or placing a cup of salt in a bucket of warm or cold water and soaking your feet for 40 minutes. Make sure the water is not discarded in the kitchen sink, where food is prepared; we don't need vegetables stained with negativity. Place salt in containers or bowls made of glass, ceramic, wood or shell, just not plastic or metal, and place under tables, beds or office desks—anywhere that seems to be an energy drain or where there are negative individuals. The negative energies will be drawn to the salt container. Empty the salt down the toilet once a week and refill.

Sage or smudge stick

We have American Indians to thank for sage's contribution to warding off negative energies. At the end of each week, I sit down with a lit sage stick, and work in an anticlockwise direction from my head to the souls of my feet. At times I feel the negative energy lift off my body's aura. For those who find sage too pungent, you can use lavender. When smudging your home or a room, have a window or door open to allow negative energies to escape. If you have spirit visitors who you wish to move on, this works wonders. Don't forget, you can also command a spirit to leave by saying, 'Please leave, and go to the light'. The use of oil burners using lavender or sage are appropriate, just watch small children near naked flames. My neighbours always know I'm awake when they smell my favourite Nag Champa incense burning—smoke dispels lower energies.

Water

At the conclusion of my reading day, I have a shower and wash my hair, allowing the water to wash away any build-up of negative energies I may have accumulated. Then I change into a complete set of clean clothes. My ironing person just loves me—he's never out of work! Residues of negative energies can be trapped in the pores of our skin and on our clothes. A glass of water will also absorb negativity: It can be a great solution for an office full of stress and can be easily left on a desk or table without anyone the wiser. Never drink this water though, or use it on plants, because you'll be allowing this negative residue to feed your body or your plants. If you're accustomed to having a drink of water by your bed, place a saucer or lid on the glass.

32

The priest and the medium

A heart needs only its own voice to do what is right.

Vanna Bonta

My eldest son, Andrew, attended a Catholic college. Early one morning, I had a very vivid dream that I had to give a message to the head teaching brother at the college. The dream quoted biblical passages, and I was to give the brother courage and confidence in his abilities as a priest. Now there was no way I was going to ring or even write to a Catholic brother and perhaps bring extreme pressure to my son who attended that school.

All through the morning, I kept hearing in my mind: 'You must deliver this message, you must'. No way, I thought. So I went shopping.

Upon my return I noticed that a portrait of Andrew in his college uniform had fallen off the picture wall. I had a whole wall full of a variety of photos of the family. No-one else had been home so I thought it was just coincidence, although deep down I was secretly thinking, 'Surely this isn't God or Spirit at work'.

I put the picture back up, did some work around the house then went out again. The house was left empty, again no-one else was home. Upon returning, I opened the front door, and jumped back, absolutely stunned and shocked. The photo of Andrew had not only come off the picture wall, it had made its way from the wall, around the corner, under the archway and was facing upwards towards the front door. I couldn't miss it!

I rang my friend, Louise, who is not into conservative religions, yet she said, 'Oh, whatever the message is to that brother, you'd better give it to him. Something's going on in your house.'

I'd cut my finger on my writing hand, quite badly. I don't have perfect writing at the best of times—no-one can ever read what I write—so I had an excuse again not to write to the brother.

It was just before 11 p.m. on Sunday, when suddenly the most intense smell of rosemary permeated through the lounge room. As rosemary signifies remembering, and is traditionally used on Anzac Day to remember our dearly departeds who fought in the wars, I had to ask myself if Spirit was trying to invoke my memory of the message with the fragrance?

Then I saw a monk walk from my kitchen, and even as a write this I'm getting goosebumps again. He seemed so real. He was dressed in a brown habit with a hood covering his head. He positioned himself at the dining room table, behind the chair I occupy when having the evening meal. I just knew I had to write to the brother with the message—obviously the monk wasn't going to go away until I had accomplished the task he was there to oversee.

I didn't own a computer back then, so with a pen and a piece of paper in hand, I wrote the message—with Andrew's photo coming off the wall twice, the fragrance and the monk standing behind me. If my son or I were going to be excommunicated from the college culture, we may as well go out in style!

The next morning, I relayed the event to the staff in the office where I worked, all five of whom were Catholic. They begged me to send the letter, although I never divulged the message, just the circumstances. They had learnt over the years never to doubt my experiences.

Some six weeks passed and I received a letter from the brother. He apologised for his lateness. In fact, he wrote that when I had the dream it was Vocation Sunday in his order. It's the day set aside for the brothers and priests to reflect upon their commitment to the church and the order, and how they saw themselves being of service in the coming years. The scriptures I had given him were ones he'd been studying.

He explained that his reason for taking time off from the college was to attend a retreat, to pray and contemplate whether he should take the next step in his spiritual life from a brother to a priest. He thanked me for this message and asked me to keep him in my prayers.

I hoped perhaps I'd given him some comfort or confirmation of his direction in life. I'm not a Catholic; I was raised as a Methodist and eventually become a Sunday school teacher. So I was totally unaware of the doctrine for brothers and priests in the Catholic faith. I felt reassured and happy when I read the official announcement in the college newsletter that he was leaving to become a priest.

My gift as a medium that day was truly tested. Was I bold enough and confident enough to move beyond my fear and deliver an important message? I'm so pleased I did—this man had been praying and asking his Heavenly Father for guidance and confirmation as to his vocation in the church. Heavenly wisdom that Sunday was delivered to a medium—me—to give to one chosen to lead and shepherd His flock. I smile as I sense the intertwining of two very different messengers—a Christian brother and me, working in the supernatural world. You could say we are divinely linked; the common thread is that we both work to deliver messages from above, that there is life after death—it's just open to interpretation!

33

Keeping an open mind

The mind has exactly the same power as the hands;
not merely to grasp the world, but to change it.

Colin Wilson

Your own belief system may start to be challenged by the shock of losing someone special. You may cling to the religion of your childhood, you may build on these beliefs, or you may pull away from structured philosophies and start looking for alternatives; and if you have never been to church before, you may now start to question whether there really is a God or Heaven. This is the gift you've been given through loss.

If you haven't already, you may start to question your own principles and those of your family, friends and culture. This is part of the evolution of your own soul's development. How fortunate you are to be able to now question your own mortality, your own purpose and direction. You may never have thought about spiritual things until your visit to a psychic medium puts you on a spiritual quest to find the answers.

Not all mediums conduct private readings. Some internationally acclaimed mediums, such as renowned psychic medium James Van Praagh, travel the world giving live performances to stadiums packed with thousands of people. This is a daunting task. Imagine all those people jammed in next to each other, sitting in the dark, while he's under a beacon of intense stage lighting, tuning into communications from the other side. This task takes great skill and experience to deliver accurately what he's receiving. No wonder at times there can be crossed lines as he channels his senses to receive.

A more informal demonstration of proof of the existence of communication from the dearly departed can be experienced at a Spiritualist church, which believes that after we die we go back into Spirit until we make the choice to return to earth. Each Sunday there's a visiting psychic medium doing 'platform work', where the medium uses their unique style and gifts to deliver messages from one's past to members of the audience, usually in a small group setting.

During the time my parents were investigating the Spiritualist movement, Mum would make meticulous notes from any messages that were received by any mediums working the platform. She would sit down when she returned home in the evening and write down everything she could remember, and still to this day she has boxes of her carefully hand-written notes with their incredible detail.

On quizzing her for suitable stories for this book regarding demonstrations from the platform to support the belief in the afterlife, one story in particular stood out in her mind—Jack's story.

'I'll have to search through the huge boxes in the back room for the story—it may take me some time to work my way through the stories, but I'll find it, and next time you visit you can take it away with you,' she said.

'Gina, you won't believe this, the first one I clapped my eyes on was Jack's story.' It was as though it had mysteriously plotted itself in a position that would be discovered immediately. The once-white foolscap paper was now a shade of coffee, and felt limp to touch in the hands. The blue biro writing had faded on the outer edges, but was still very readable.

Mum started telling me that Albert Best, the Scottish medium, was said to be the best in the UK at that time. Albert had received a number of visits from Anne, the deceased wife of a retired Church of England minister. Anne had given Albert such accurate and detailed information that he was able to track down her husband and give him the messages. Anne was concerned that he was depressed, sad and drinking too much. She even told the medium where she had placed his clean clerical collar—a simple message, but understandably natural for a wife. Her continued appearances would eventually convince this retired minister of life after death. He went on to write a book, *A Venture in Immortality*.

The demonstration

We went to a demonstration at a nearby Town Hall, a good hour's drive away. There were hundreds present. Dad was lucky enough to have some messages via Albert Best as well.

During the evening Albert pointed to Dad in the audience. 'I am coming to you—the man with his hand under his chin. I have a man here with a strong accent, he's Geordie. His name is Jack. I am reminded of the times when Jack and you had a few drinks.'

Dad didn't drink, but when he visited Jack they'd have a cup of coffee.

'I get County Durham and also a connection with Newcastle. Does that mean anything to you?' Albert asked.

'Possibly,' Dad replied. Mum and Dad didn't believe in feeding the medium too much detail—they were there to receive, not to divulge!

Albert continued, 'He was a singer and he's singing a song for you—'The Bladen Races'. [This was a song particular to that region of Newcastle in England.]

'I look at you and I hear Burslem and Tunstall, Fenton, Longton and names like that. [All these towns were from the pottery area where Dad grew up.]

'With you, sir, I get the phrase: "Go kick a bow against a wa." [This is an old-fashioned Staffordshire way of talking. It meant: 'Go kick a ball against a wall.']

'Could you say that for me now, sir?'

'I couldn't speak like that now,' Dad replied.

'Never mind, we'll go back to Jack, your friend,' Albert went on. 'Well sir, your friend is happy to make this link, and he thinks of you all the time. He can tell you could accept everything, and he indicates how happy it made him feel.'

Mum had written a summary of the day's demonstration: 'This story was told for two reasons: 1. To share a healing story with you all, to encourage you. 2. To comfort you, for times of loss of loved ones. This man proved to me that he still lives. Life goes on, in the Spirit world.'

In due course, my mum would work on the platform for many years, delivering messages of hope and proof of the existence of life after death.

Searching for the Truth

Investigating 'the truth' can be rewarding. You may refer to yourself as a Christian, Muslim or Jew, or align yourself with another faith. If you attend a Spiritualist or New Age demonstration, you'll come across a varied group of individuals with varying gifts, talents and philosophies.

Go with an open mind—treat it like a smorgasbord at a restaurant, where you have choices. You can sample the entrees, indulge in many courses and feast on the desserts. How much you eat and digest is up to you. So too, choose with discernment what you see, hear and observe that day. If your intuition is tugging at you, and saying, 'All is not right here', be on guard! Not everyone works to the glory of the most high.

In the early days of my parents' investigation into the Spiritualist movement, they withdrew from a church they had started visiting when they heard the male clairvoyant had been arrested for theft. While the clients were waiting in the church for their readings, he was off robbing their homes!

The quality and content of communication can differ greatly from service to service and from group to group. Are there highly trained teachers who can guide and instruct you? Ask yourself, is this a place of comfort and peace? Is my spiritual journey developing, unfolding? Am I developing my spiritual path? Be on guard if you hear people making promises, guarantees of communicating with the afterlife.

Some of you may investigate and join a development circle where like-minded people meet to develop their natural psychic abilities and learn how to expand their energy and access the spirit realms. Usually, these circles meet once a week in the same location with a leader who is experienced in mediumship development.

Through loss, we are often placed on our true soul's purpose, and I have known people who have become excellent mediums through their own personal tragedy of loss of a loved one.

I can guarantee one thing, your beloved will be excited that you are searching for the truth, that you seeking to have some understanding or even now have achieved some belief that they have made the transition to the other side. They will be eagerly waiting to communicate with you—and it just may be through a psychic medium!

34

Signs and messages

The meeting of two personalities is like the contact of
two chemical substances: if there is any reaction,
both are transformed.

Carl Jung

Working as a psychic medium is one of the most
rewarding and fulfilling aspects of my gift. To communicate and relay messages from the other side is my
reward. It hasn't been easy though. Just imagine trying to understand someone speaking to you in a foreign language—one you're
not familiar with. Sometimes the expressions on their face and the
way they use their hands can be more valuable in comprehending
the message than the actual words they're using. You know how
draining this can be. So when a psychic medium contacts someone
who has passed over, both will find the exchange of information
energetically draining.

Messages are not fluid like earthly communications. They often
stop and start. As Spirit becomes depleted of strength, they pull

back to gather more momentum, then rally to continue with the session. Have patience with the medium, as they too will expend much of their own energy trying to tap into this field.

Clients are sometimes frustrated with the messages relayed from the other side, believing them trivial. Remember, your loved one's personality doesn't become angelic just because they're in heaven. If they were a grumbly old man in this life, the messages may come through in the same tone. You're dealing with real-life characters who have made a transition to another place, another tomorrow, continuing with their own unique identities. Some may refer to high points in their life, events and circumstances you were not aware of, for example, winning the Country Cricket Cup or making ginger beer stored under their grandmother's house. You may well need to become an investigator to track down the relevance of this information.

I just love it when I receive an email or a telephone call from a client who can't place some of the information relayed at their reading only to do research and have accurate feedback from associates that the information was indeed factual after all.

When conducting a psychic reading, I see symbols and receive information in a variety of forms. I have learnt to say what I see, hear and feel. This doesn't mean that my interpretation of the images will always be correct. Mediums can misinterpret the pictures, symbols and signs.

I recall a woman in Spirit pointing to her eye, then she touched her heart and then she showed me a sheep with a lamb. So my interpretation was maybe someone was connected to a rural setting and she had a vision and heart problem. But the young man having the reading saw it completely differently. He told me his grandmother, when alive, had a particular loving way of communicating with him using her type of 'sign language'. She would point to her eye, then her heart and then point to him. In fact what she was trying to convey was 'I love you'. The sheep was an ewe. He knew exactly what she was trying to say.

Let's take another example. I felt great pain in my right breast while communicating with a woman on the other side, and she kept pointing to her breast and then pointing to the woman having the reading. I felt she must have passed over with breast cancer. Later I was to learn that the woman having the reading had just been diagnosed with breast cancer in the same breast. It was her sister in spirit wanting her to know she was aware of her current health diagnosis.

Having a misinterpretation doesn't mean we are off course and not communicating thoroughly with the other side, it's just that we need loads of patience and determination to work through the newly formed 'spirit language'.

Spirit communicates through thought, called 'telepathy', and I read these thoughts. This is called 'mental mediumship'. The thoughts may be in a picture, a song or a movie, feelings in my body, a taste sensation in my mouth, a particular fragrance, smell or sometimes a sound. The information comes through very quickly—sometimes simultaneously—and I pick up speed with my own talking as I try to disseminate the symbols to my client.

Being able to draw on my own life experience allows me to have a deeper understanding and interpretation of what is being given.

In touch with loved ones

By now you must be asking yourself: 'How will I know when my dearly departed is communicating with me?' Many clients are so disappointed not to have had some sign from their loved one. Upon questioning their expectations, they often refer to scenes from movies such as the *The Sixth Sense* or *Dragonfly*. Wanting an experience so vivid and out of this world, they won't be able to discard the signs of a supernatural experience. Take the pressure off yourself. It's highly unlikely your bedclothes will be pulled from you, snow fall in your lounge room during summer, or the furniture will rearrange itself overnight—Spirit is subtle!

You would be wise in asking yourself: 'How do I know that what I am experiencing is genuine, real and not wishful thinking or imagination?' I receive hundreds of letters and emails weekly from all over the world from people looking for answers to explain unusual experiences or events they believe could be from their dearly departed. Philippa wrote to me after she and her daughter had some unusual experiences of this kind. She was puzzled and seeking an explanation for the happenings that had occurred in two different households:

My husband Ian passed on four years ago. I began hearing a loud yelling voice in my right ear saying, 'No, no, no, Philippa' and 'I love you' at various quiet times. One night I awoke at 2 a.m., 4 a.m. and 6 a.m. on the dot, followed by swirling grey clouds behind my eyes, vanishing into a woman in an oval frame. The woman had straight hair and a thin mouth, and was wearing a Dutch hat and a high neckline.

The next morning my daughter arrived from country Victoria to spend two days here. She told me she had awakened at precisely the same times as I had the previous night. She had brought her husband's family album with her. It started in the 1700s, and in it was pictured the woman I'd seen that morning. She was born in the early 1800s.

Several weeks ago I awoke from a fifteen-minute catnap and Ian was standing near my chair, looking thin and tall, wearing a blue checked shirt (he never actually owned one), and long pants, with swirling clouds moving around his lower legs. I stared at him without blinking for approximately seven seconds before he vanished. I'm perplexed. Is there an explanation for these happenings?

I sense Philippa may have doubted these signs from Spirit if it wasn't for the fact that her daughter awoke at the same times. So what was happening for Philippa? I believe the woman in the family album was a bonus. It would be immediate proof of the afterlife when she flicked through the pages of the family photo album to find the woman's photo. Spirit, too, wants to validate their existence in the afterlife. I would suggest next time Philippa sees a spirit vanish into a frame, she should investigate other photo albums or pictures as this is the 'Language of Spirit' trying to use photos as subtle clues that grab her attention; giving her a message that she and her family are being guided, looked after, thought about.

Her husband's words, 'No, no, no, Philippa' and 'I love you' convey his need to communicate to her his feelings—that love endures all physical separation. Although the physical body has died, the soul lives on; some call this Spirit, angels or guides. Love is enduring, it is everlasting. Just as the living have free will to change clothes, and our physical appearances alter from month to year, our beloveds go through the same transitional phases where they can manipulate their energy to bring an altered state of appearance.

Of the thousands of recounted stories I have read and been told, many have occurred just as the person woke up from sleep or at quiet times. It is at these times the Language of Spirit is more easily accessible to many—when we allow our conscious mind to shut down, opening a link between the body and mind.

Learning to communicate with Spirit may be easy for some, while others strain as they try to attract Spirit communication. Don't get upset and worried. After all, it's unfamiliar territory. Learning a new language takes time. Some will progress rapidly and others may take years to finally be able to tune in and receive or notice the little clues left by Spirit. But you will improve as you learn the subtleties of their language. The feather or coin you find now becomes a message: 'I'm thinking of you.' A whiff of fragrance, flowers or food now transports you to a memory shared together. You are finally starting to acknowledge and open your senses to a new way of communicating with Spirit.

Craig and Tania were waiting for the traffic lights to change, when they both felt an icy cold feeling enter the car. They looked at each other, frightened, when Craig sighted out of the corner of his eye the cemetery where Tania's grandfather had been buried several months before. They felt sure it was his way of communicating.

Passing over to the other side becomes a new learning field for your dearly departed as well. Recall how the astronauts had to learn to walk in space with no gravitational pull; eventually a new style and method was developed so they could walk on the moon. They needed to adjust and train to become attuned to a new way of acting, moving and thinking in their unfamiliar new environment. So this is true for your loved one on the other side.

A question I'm repeatedly asked in my sessions is, 'Is he with me, looking after me all the time?' You may not like the answer. It is yes and no. Most certainly your loved one has the desire to assist and be with you as much as possible; however, just as you are reading this book, some of your friends and family are off doing their own activities. Your loved one will at times be with other important people in their lives on the other side. Wouldn't you want the best and most loving care to be given to those in need?

Sometimes spirit communicates in dramatic ways. My son, Andrew, while working in the UK, scored a temporary nightclub manager's position. One particular evening, a patron was under the influence of what appeared to be alcohol and drugs. Needing to separate him from the other patrons, Andrew coaxed him towards his office. Unfortunately, none of the staff were aware of what was happening. Suddenly the customer grabbed a bottle, smashed it against the wall and took it to my son's throat. It was a life and death situation.

My deceased father manifested in front of Andrew, telling him to say the words: 'What would it prove?' Over and over, my father continued to tell Andrew what else to say to get control of the situation.

Gradually the man withdrew the bottle and calmed down. Relieved he had escaped with his life, but emotional after his experience, Andrew tried to call me but was unable to reach me, so he rang my mother. He told his nan, 'Pa just came and saved me.'

Divine protection from beyond the grave came through that day. However, we are often misled, believing that those we love in the afterlife are watching over us 24/7. This is not the case; they have free will and sometimes there are greater challenges and victories they are to perform.

Sometimes people get a lot of messages from Spirit, sometimes not. My dad has been gone nearly twelve years and to this day, I have only seen him six times since his death, and my mum has seen him about the same number of times. So even having an established gift doesn't necessarily mean we are more privileged than others to have access to the individuals we cherish. We realise my dad is doing what he needs to do. His visit to Andrew gave us comfort that he is still carrying out his mission of family protector, be it from another dimension. It is comforting to realise that our ancestors are often our guides.

A word of caution here—don't do foolish things thinking that your loved one will stop you making mistakes or protect you in dangerous situations. You've been given free will and the ability to make your own decisions and choices. Your loved one can see your blueprint of the soul, and knows quite definitely what lies ahead for you now they are back in Spirit. But sometimes they can't stop lessons and circumstances from happening.

As a loving soul they have to step back and allow you to continue on your mission in this life, just as a parent sees the struggle of their crawling baby learning to pull himself up on furniture to try and take his first steps at independence only to fall and perhaps hurt himself. They know if they continually rush to their baby's aid, he will never confidently be able to learn to walk by himself. So they stand back, and cheer and clap with much love as he struggles, knowing ultimately the end result will be achieved.

You can feel confident and know that Spirit is replicating the same love; however, they know 'the bigger picture' ahead for you, and that some things are well and truly out of their control. It is your karmic path!

35

Dream power

Millions of spiritual creatures walk this earth unseen,
both when we sleep and when we are awake.

John Milton

Kerrie was very close to her grandmother, and when she passed over she left her antique wrought iron bed as a legacy to remember their times together reading stories and sharing experiences. It was not uncommon for Kerrie to have visits in her dreams from Grandma reminding her of cherished moments they shared. One such dream wasn't so comforting though—it left Kerrie confused and questioning what it meant.

Kerrie and I met through our seven-year-old sons. Although the boys were now nearing their 21st birthdays, we still spoke nearly every day on the phone. It was during one of these calls that Kerrie told about her grandma's visit and the subsequent dream. In it, she showed Kerrie a tree that had little birds frozen in what looked like plastic bags. Grandma took one plastic bag off the tree and allowed it to thaw next to a pond with fish swimming in it.

'I just can't work this one out, can you Georgina?'

'Kerrie—it's a pregnancy dream. She's indicating the fish are the sperm and the frozen bird is an egg.'

Kerrie laughed. At 42, pregnancy was the last thing on her mind. 'Impossible,' she said.

Months passed, and I returned from overseas to hear that Kerrie had taken ill at a conference interstate. On her return home, her doctor took blood tests for further investigation. The phone rang, and it was her doctor.

'I need to see you immediately—you're at least six weeks pregnant.'

In shock, Kerrie and her partner rushed to see the doctor. The scan not only revealed she was pregnant, but five months pregnant. Grandma's visit to Kerrie was telling her she was pregnant.

Four months later, Olivia-Charlotte entered the world. Her conception heralded by her great-grandmother in Spirit and—we believe—divinely sent!

Many such dreams come in the period between sleep and wakefulness. Perhaps this is a porthole between the busyness of the mind and sleep; a time when you're more receptive to a message.

Yes, some dreams can be replays of the day's activities, fears and problems you are going over in your subconscious mind. You may wake feeling drained, unsure of what you have experienced in your dream state. However, a prophetic or dearly departed dream has clarity, is often seen in colour and is recalled with some degree of ease of experience.

Some people say it feels as though they were awake and having a conversation or witnessing an event first-hand, or they may be given a literal image or phrase in their dream, one that will jog their memory recall. Lindy dreamt of the Easter bunny calling out, 'Holiday, holiday!' You may well think as Lindy did that the dream was telling her to have a holiday during the Easter break. Later that week, down at the local shops, she saw someone dressed in a bunny suit handing out brochures for a holiday.

It occurred just as she had dreamt it. If only one aspect of her dream later transpires in real life, like seeing someone dressed as the Easter bunny or hearing someone call out 'Holiday, holiday!', then her dream qualifies as a literal dream (one that is so clear and concise in detail the message is obvious). Some dreams, like Kerrie's, use symbols that are open to interpretation.

There is a great array of dream interpretation books in the marketplace. On comparison, you will note that sometimes they differ with interpretation of symbols. I suggest, as I have done over the years, you start to record your dreams on the computer or in an exercise book. Leave space for additions as you start to unravel your own symbolism and interpretation. The use of symbols is very personal. Try contemplating any previous association with that image or feeling.

I find that writing down what you have seen or felt can activate your own divine intuition and more interpretations can flow from this exercise. Dreams can be guide posts to events in your life. However, be wary of trying to manipulate or force the interpretation to fit what you would like to see happen. On the other hand, if you take an attitude of denial and try to push away the message you don't want to acknowledge, your inner wisdom will keeping drawing you back to look at a more obvious choice.

Symbols are Spirit's shortcuts to message imprinting. When you learn your own unique Language of Spirit through symbols, you will have no doubt or confusion as to what the dream means to you. By using this technique, I have discovered—with much surprise—that every time I dream of Arnold Schwarzenegger from *Terminator*, for example, there's a significant change in my future. You may recall the theme from this series of movies was about a robot that could change the course of the future. So for me, that's what Arnie stands for, while for someone else he may signify strength.

I wouldn't have seen the thread linking these random dreams together unless I had noted what was occurring in my life at that time. If you have a trusted friend, sharing the dream, as Kerrie did with me, may assist in deciphering the cryptic clues. A friend may have a greater understanding and a more objective viewpoint of where you stand in your life and your circumstances at a given time.

Prophetic dreams foretell an event to come. I recall dreaming that I was speaking to two men of different nationalities, and they both turned to me and said: 'If you put your resume in, we'll give you the job'. I'd been thinking about applying for a job the previous week, but concluded I didn't have all the essential and desirable attributes to score an interview. Yet the dream gave me confidence to try.

I had one day to retype my resume and apply for the position. I was interviewed, and offered the position! It was that very job that led to me uncovering corruption years later that in turn led to me working as a full-time psychic. If I hadn't had that initial dream and followed it through, I may not be writing this book right now!

Higher wisdom through dreams

There's a practical technique I teach in my psychic development workshops whereby students can learn to program their subconscious minds prior to sleep. It's easy and has great results. Just as you're about to go to bed, make sure you have your note book and pen at your bedside. Now think of a question you'd like answered. It must be one question only, and not, 'Tell me the Lotto numbers for next week, what should I spend the money on and when do you think I should purchase the new house?' This exercise is about training yourself and your spirit guides to work in unison. It's not about confusing both worlds. A suitable question would be, 'When should I purchase a new house?'

Write the question on a piece of paper. The question should be the last thing on your mind when you hop into bed.

A word of caution—I don't want to create disharmony in the marital bed, so you may need to explain to your partner that you're unavailable as you're working on a spiritual practice. As you get comfortable in your bed, think over again the question you've just written down. Now spell in your mind or aloud the word 'dream'—

you must spell not say it—i.e. D—R—E—A—M, and keep up this mantra until you fall asleep. It's much like counting sheep.

Upon waking, whether it's during the night or in the morning, note any feelings you have—good, bad, happy, sad, etc.—and note any visions, sounds or information that may have come to you during the night. Record all this information on your computer or in an exercise book. No matter how trivial the information seems, keep a record. Spirit may give you many clues each night, like a puzzle.

If you get an answer the first night, you're very lucky! Don't be disheartened if you don't, or if you haven't remembered any. This is all about training yourself. Remember how hard it was to learn how to drive a car or use a computer—you thought you'd never get the hang of it, but now you operate almost on autopilot. The same is to be said about this exercise. Continue for seven nights, of course to be abandoned if you receive your answer beforehand.

After seven nights without a significant result, put the exercise aside for a week and recommence the exercise with a different question. Some prayers are not answered, as divine timing and divine selection are part of our karmic experience. With enough dedication and practice, you will be able to retrieve higher wisdom and answers to your questions. Can you recall a time when you rang to speak to a particular friend or family member, only to have someone else pick up the receiver armed with the answer you were seeking?

Spirit operates in the same way. You issue a prayer, a demand or a request for a particular loved one to give you guidance, but in the wisdom of Spirit, the request may be diverted to someone more proficient, wise or appropriate. I call this divine wisdom. So don't be disheartened if you ask to receive a message from someone special, only to have it substituted with another guide or more relevant source. Trust that you are being divinely inspired and guided.

36

Wisdom of the inner voice

Where there is no vision, the people perish.
The Bible, Proverbs, Chapter 29, Verse 18

Your vivid and prophetic dreams just don't happen during the night; the short catnap you take in the afternoon can produce startling insights. Many of the world's research scientists, physicists, film directors, composers, writers and artists have developed inventions and concepts while they daydreamed. They have tapped into a hidden source of power and wisdom—the inner voice.

Thoughts that pop into your head

Helen was engrossed in her daily data entry work when suddenly thoughts of her son Michael flashed into her head. She imagined him lying on the lounge doubled up in pain. There was no reason to have this thought—it was school holidays and Michael was a trustworthy fifteen-year-old who always consulted her if there was a problem. Besides, he wasn't sick that morning when she left, and he hadn't rung to say he was feeling ill.

She tried to talk herself out of worrying, but her sense of fear got worse. She rang home to make sure he was okay, but the phone just rang out. She thought it strange, because he always told her if he planned to go out. (This was in the days before everyone carried a mobile phone.) Then she felt an overwhelming thought: 'Something's wrong with Michael.' No-one was telling her this, it was a thought, an inspirational thought—but from where? She just knew it was a thought she couldn't dismiss.

She quickly retrieved her belongings from her locker at work, and the usual fifteen-minute trip home only took ten. She got all the green traffic lights—which never usually happened, but thankfully that day luck was on her side. Racing up the back stairs to her apartment above the butcher's shop, she pushed open the door to see Michael delirious on the lounge. She rang for an ambulance, which arrived in just under ten minutes as it was stationed in the same suburb. Within an hour, Michael was in the operating theatre.

'Your son had ruptured appendicitis—he nearly died. It was very lucky for him you made it here in time,' the surgeon explained to Helen.

Everyone has thoughts that pop into their heads; some call them gut feelings or hunches. My friend Louise's husband, Neil, is a real sceptic about my abilities. He sells farm machinery to 'practical, real men'—or so he thinks! I was visiting their rural home when one evening, while we were sitting at the dining room table having our evening meal, he jumped up and said, 'I've got to make a phone call. If I don't close this deal, I'll lose him, [meaning closing the sale for the machinery]. He later returned to the table with a smile on his face—he'd clinched the deal. I asked him why he suddenly had to make that call. He laughed, 'It's not that stuff you do, Georgina. It just came to me that I needed to make that call there and then.' I rest my case.

Inspiration, they say, can manifest out of the blue as an idea or a thought. Actually, inspiration means 'in spirit'. Yes, we are being divinely guided. We can learn to tap into the energy of inspiration. Have you ever finished the sentence of a friend—maybe you telepathically read their thoughts? This is how Spirit communicates with a medium and now yourself, through 'in-Spirational' thought. Have you ever rung a friend because their name suddenly came to you in thought, only to hear they were just about to dial your number? I bet you have. This is also how the world of Spirit communication occurs. Through the power of thought, they will try to get your attention.

Learning to meditate or relax assists your mind to learn the craft of 'stillness'. This allows you to actively close off the chatty-ness of your mind to become open to receive inspiration and clear reception from the afterlife. For others, stillness can be quietly working away at a craft or a hobby—something they love. I have clients who say, 'When I paint I just get lost in the moment.' Some say they feel the presence of their loved one with them. They can't see anything, they just have a feeling. The stillness has allowed their senses to fine-tune their receptor channels.

37

Getting in touch

Reduce your plan to writing. The moment you
complete this, you will have definitely given concrete
form to the intangible desire.

Napoleon Hill

The world of Spirit communication is open to everybody. It's
a matter of trial and error until you find the tool that works
best for you. Ezra was a frustrated writer, successful as a
sub-editor in the magazine industry, yet she longed to write a
novel about her grandfather's time as a missionary. Sitting at home
in front of her computer screen only ever resulted in several pages
of work—writer's block was impeding the flow of creativity.

'What am I doing wrong, Georgina?' she asked. 'I remember
in one of your workshops you mentioned a technique called
automatic writing. Do you reckon it would work while using a
computer, rather than just handwriting?' Relearning the technique,
within several weeks Ezra had made huge progress with the manuscript, all logged on her computer.

Looking back, she was blown away with the fine detail she seemed to channel from another source—the source I called 'divine wisdom'. By opening herself to Spirit communication and wisdom, Ezra let go of tension, and divine energy and wisdom was channelled through her fingertips. We both knew Spirit had come to her rescue.

Automatic writing

A wonderful way to train your inspirational communication is with a pen and writing pad or your computer and keyboard. Many of my students love this technique, as it's straightforward and easy to master. As you practise the technique, the channels of communication will become more open. People often associate automatic writing with séances and spirit possession. For some intuitives, this has became an accurate way of accessing Spirit communication, but what I'm teaching here is more practical and easier to achieve results.

Before commencing the exercise, consider what you're seeking from Spirit. Like the dream exercise, you'll need to formulate one question. It may be a message from your dearly departed, for example: 'Am I doing the right thing about the headstone?' or, 'Dad—I need to know if you're happy.' Once you've decided upon a question, you'll need to have on hand a large note pad with several pens or be sitting at the ready in front of your computer. Have you used a psychic protection routine today? If not, most definitely apply one now.

Find yourself a quiet spot, perhaps a special corner in your house where you can't be disturbed. Switch off all phones. For some, the garden, sitting in the car by the beach or overlooking a beautiful mountain landscape will provide a source of bliss—as long as you're comfortable. Think calm, relaxation, peacefulness. For those who are using pen and paper, have several pens on standby— you won't want to run out. Now, take a deep breath in . . . and out . . . repeat this process about nine times. Don't get stressed if you lose count and do eleven, or seven; this is just about learning to set the scene, the foundation for your inspirational thought.

Next, write your question at the top of the page. Under your question, write these words: 'What is it that I need to know?' Immediately start writing whatever comes to your mind in thoughts or feelings. Maybe you get a waft of breeze or a fragrance from a flower bed. Write that down. Don't read, question or pull apart what you've written. Just keep writing. Don't analyse or rationalise what you're writing down. Just keep writing. If you get writer's block, write down your question again and repeat the entire process. Do this again and again. The things you've written may seem like nonsense and you may be frustrated, but remember—we're dealing with the Language of Spirit. There are no translators here to assist you, so you have to learn to deal with the chattiness before you can receive clear reception.

For some, the first attempt can bring significant results. As they start to pore over the information, key words and phrases jump out; colours have significance and scenes start to formulate. For others, it seems a waste of time. Consider what your incentive was to get your car licence. Was it mobility, or freedom to access places you normally couldn't? This exercise will transport your thoughts to receive information that may have been previously unavailable. By reading over the pages, you may find you've been given a totally different concept or message than you expected.

Keep all your notes, as you may find over time that there is a theme, a prophecy or a message on issues that may arise in the future. When you feel that you've done enough, you may wish to say a silent thank you and goodbye to Spirit until your next appointment. It's essential that you start to learn to activate and close each session. This work can be exhilarating, but also draining. Your guides need to know when to switch on and when to switch off. It doesn't mean you're stopping them from contacting you, but you do have earthly responsibilities to attend to and you need to become grounded again.

In summary, you need to find a quiet place, adopt a psychic protection ritual, commence the session with slow, deep breaths, then ask your question, waiting for the answer to flow. Always end a session with a closure technique.

Messages out of thin air

The wonderful world of Spirit is very imaginative, and will always find a way to catch your attention to deliver a message. They can manipulate air and energy, delivering objects that seem to appear out of thin air. They are usually small items such as flowers, gems or stones, or even ancient coins and jewellery, and are believed to come from what we call the 'fourth dimension'. These items are referred to as 'apports'.

Brigette always left her car keys in a glass bowl that sat at the entrance to the front door, it was an automatic function and she'd done it for years. Soon after her father died, she started to discover the keys in different places throughout her home. Sometimes they'd be at the front door, other times next to her shoes. It was during her reading that her beloved dad declared he'd been up to mischief and hoped she could see the funny side of his actions.

She was relieved—she wasn't going mad, it was just her dad letting her know he was around. Signs from the other side are sometimes very difficult to comprehend, but nevertheless they are gifts to let us know we're not alone.

Another type of physical contact Spirit can manifest can be through electrical activity. In a Dearly Departed reading, one of my clients wanted to reach his mum. She showed me a scene in her kitchen, most definitely her domain before she died, and I could see lightbulbs blowing out.

Her son told me that when she died he had replaced three light globes in the kitchen, one after the other had blown. She knew exactly how to grab his attention. His mother kept showing me the number '66'. But the message didn't make sense until several nights later when he heard a message being left on his mobile phone. Picking up the phone from his bedside table, a cold shiver went down his spine as he saw it showed a full screen of number sixes.

I've had clients whose televisions or radios suddenly turn on by themselves. In fact, I've replaced two digital clock radios in my bedroom recently—different brands from different shops. They kept going too fast, sometimes hours ahead! I discussed this with one of my very gifted students, Louise, who is a scientist, and she hypothesised that due to my intense prophetic dreams, I could literally be moving forward in time, and somehow altering the magnetic fields of the clocks.

The American Association of Electronic Voice Phenomena believes it has thousands of cases where voices can be heard on magnetic tapes such as cassettes and answering machines. Louise has had great success on her many travels both local and internationally when taking random photographs of interesting scenes, tourist sites and spiritual places to discover when scanning her holiday snaps she had captured superimposed faces. One in particular she showed me was taken near a sacred Hindu site in India, and the image captured was that of an ancient Hindu goddess.

Sometimes you may see balls of light called 'orbs' in your photos, indicating Spirit's presence. Perhaps there's something to be said of the speed of light and the way the camera can capture what the naked eye finds difficult to see.

A former colleague of mine came to work much shaken one morning. The telephone had rung at about 4 a.m. at her brother's home, and fearing it may have been bad news about his aged mother, he jumped up to answer it. When he got to the phone, no-one was there. Concerned the ringing may have woken their young baby, he went into the baby's room to see if he was disturbed, only to discover he'd stopped breathing. The father frantically tried to revive the child, with no success. The diagnosis was sudden infant death syndrome.

So why did the telephone ring? Was it a call to heaven; the parting of the baby's soul bidding a fond farewell to his parents and alerting heaven that he was on his way? I know the phone call made the father realise that the child's fate was out of his hands, even though he had tried his hardest to save him. We may never know the real reason the call came, but I would like to think it was a call to heaven.

I've known others to receive a telephone call or listen to their answering machine only to pick up a very faint voice with background static. Spirit has been known to knock on doors or walls and create clapping noises to grab people's attention.

When my dear friend Simon passed away at 44, it was a great loss. He had opened many doors in the entertainment field for me, and in the dark days had given me a ray of sunshine and hope. I recall dreaming of Simon one night, and in the dream I had an intense rushing noise in my ear, as though I had a huge wave of ocean rushing into my ear canal. I awoke suddenly to a clapping noise in the corner, wondering whether I had a burglar in my bedroom. Then I heard it again. I pushed the covers back and switched on my bedside light, my heart pounding as I peered into the corner of my bedroom. That whole wall is wardrobes, but inside one is the switchboard that operates the electrical circuit for the apartment.

Then I saw my cat, Miracle, who sleeps on the end of my bed. She was standing up, and facing in the same direction where I heard the clapping—her back was arched and her fur standing on end. Interestingly, Simon was afraid of cats, and Miracle always sensed this and would respond to him in a nervous way. I have no doubt that my dream was the manifestation of Simon's presence. My dream heralded his arrival, and the power box was his power source.

Have you woken to find your house keys were not where you left them, only to find them somewhere else? Or lost a ring and have it turn up several months later in the same spot? How can this happen? We're all matter and have electromagnetic energy fields. I suspect Spirit have the natural ability to manipulate these energy fields to their advantage.

Many people have seen a ghost, sometimes referred to as an 'apparition', and some are very fearful of having an encounter with a ghost. I saw my father walk through the side door, dressed in his naval uniform, and next to him stood his brother and father, also dressed in wartime uniforms. They were positioning themselves behind a coffin in a funeral home. The strange thing was that the person inside the coffin was my father. Maybe this was a sign of respect for my mother. Mum never saw what I saw. I was very privileged that day. It's thought that an apparition is a recently departed spirit who hasn't completely made the transition to the afterlife due to concern for those they've left behind.

Please know that your departed loved ones do want to make their presence known and felt to you. Don't be too hard on yourself if you haven't picked up on their subtle clues to date—why not try some of my suggestions?

38

When pets die

The animal shall not be measured by man. In a world
older and more complete than ours they move
finished and completed, gifted with extensions of the
senses we have lost or never attained, living by voices
we shall never hear. They are not brethren, they are
not underlings; they are other nations, caught with
ourselves in the net of life and time.

Henry Beston, *The Outermost House*

Remember the catchy tune 'Talk to the Animals' from the movie *Dr Dolittle*? The amazing doctor seemed to exhibit paranormal abilities that enabled him to communicate with animals. Stop for a moment and consider how you communicate with your pet. Can you recall an instance when your pet seemed to be reading your mind? Perhaps your dog picked up its lead when you were only thinking of going for a walk, or maybe you noticed they were sitting at the front door ten minutes before your partner walked through the door earlier than anticipated—they knew. But how?

Why did the elephants and dogs in Phuket, Thailand, move to higher ground prior to the tsunami's devastating arrival to the mainland? Some zoos in earthquake areas have noted significant behavioural changes in their animals prior to an earthquake. Michelle, a client, used to live and work in Japan, and she told me that many of the Japanese households especially keep carp or goldfish in their homes as earthquake 'detectors'. Originally the fish were intended to bring good fortune to the households, but over many years it had been noted by their owners that prior to an earthquake the behaviour of the fish became erratic—they would rush backwards and forwards in their tank or pool. This would happen 24 hours to a week before an earthquake hit, giving their owners warning and time to implement safety procedures.

My dear friend Peter, proud of his Greek heritage, tells a story which has been passed down in his family for many years, of the Ancient Greeks' belief that there lies a connection between unusual animal behaviour and earthquakes. They believed it was form of 'secret knowledge'. Is this secret knowledge to do with the fact that all animals are psychic? They all have a well-honed sixth sense—a survival mechanism built in from conception that allows them to intuitively sense danger and changes in the environment for survival.

You were born with the same ability; however, through conditioning of family, religion or society, you were continually told 'don't be stupid', 'don't say things like that', and you learnt to shut down your natural intuitive abilities. Pet owners know the joy of being loved by their special pet. No matter how grumpy, sad or happy we are, they respond with enthusiasm and love. They love us unconditionally—warts and all.

I was transfixed when I heard the story of an old gentleman who had collapsed in his home. Lying on the floor, he was unable to move or call for help and he had resigned himself to his fate. Yet his faithful dog intuitively understood what his master needed to live. He found a towel and dipped it repeatedly into the toilet bowl, then dropped the wet towel on his owner's face so he was able to suck the moisture out and sustain himself until the pair were discovered and saved.

My children's dachshund, Rocky, intuitively warned me of impending danger when a new male staff member called around to my house. When I opened the door to let him in, Rocky flew under my bed, shaking and barking. He was a gregarious pet, and this behaviour was out of character. Even the visitor commented, 'No animal has done that to me before.' Rocky's actions alerted to me to be on guard. Something wasn't right. Later, through extensive research, I discovered that the man was a suspected paedophile who had slipped through the usual channels in the interview process and was working with disadvantaged youth. Through my dog's actions, a potential threat to the safety of youth and perhaps my own children had been avoided. His employment ceased immediately.

Animals connect with our soul; they are part of our soul's connection and the soul's journey. With their passing, their soul will go through the same stages as a human's—they still wish to comfort and support their master, say a final farewell, let their loved ones know they're okay and that they've made the transition to the other side and linked up with family members or other animals they knew or loved.

The final farewell

Teagan was an apricot long-hair Persian cat my son Andrew owned. She had one male kitten that we gave to my parents who lived a six-hour drive away from our home. They called him Winston. While my children and I were holidaying in another state, my neighbour was overseeing the care of our animals. One day my mother was in her kitchen when she turned and saw Teagan. This was impossible—Teagan was hundreds of kilometres away. But to Mum it seemed as real as though she was actually in her home. Then she disappeared as quickly as she had appeared.

On returning from our holiday, our neighbour told us Teagan had died. When Mum heard the story, she knew the cat had come to say goodbye to her kitten. It was reassuring and a lesson for the whole family, especially the children, to understand that animals too can visit from the other side and make a lasting impression on their owners.

Not everyone is gifted with clairvoyance, or clear seeing, as was my mum's experience. So how do you know your pet is connecting with you or sending you a message? There are many gifted psychics who feel comfortable working with pet communication. Again seek a referral to know you are experiencing a genuine encounter. Pets will indicate pictures and smells to a psychic, and convey a 'knowing' of what message they want to tell you—it is their form of telepathic communication. When they looked you right in the eyes and you read their thoughts, 'I'm hungry, feed me,' or 'I want to go outside, take me', through their eyes and actions, so too this is how they will communicate in Spirit to the psychic medium or to you. Be observant, and trust they will make the bridge for the connection to occur.

I recall a very distressed client showing me a photo of herself and a very big dog. All I knew was the dog had died. As I held the photo and closed my eyes, I had a vision of the dog laying on a veterinary table, the woman holding his paw as he was given an injection to go to sleep. I felt a beautiful calmness in the dog, and a sense of forgiveness and him wanting to lick her face, as if to say, 'All is well, all is forgiven, and you did the right thing'. Upon opening my eyes, I saw that the woman was one minute crying and then smiling. The dog belonged to a neighbour, who had handed her the responsibility of overseeing his care while they were away. A special closeness and bond had developed between them. He had touched her heart in his own way.

Then he was accused of biting a child. The responsibility now weighed heavily on her shoulders; although there was a unique bond, she was left with no other option but to have him put to sleep. She was devastated. This reading gave her a sense of comfort, a point of closure and a final farewell to an animal that had given her much joy, happiness and affection. A gentle giant to love!

After losing a pet, it's not uncommon to think you've heard the sound of your dog scratching at the back door or your cat's bell jingling in the hallway. Suddenly you may get that doggy smell in a particular room. Your pet's spirit will try and grab your attention and let you know that they're around; often in the same familiar soothing ways as you affectionately remembered them. Just as your pet comforted you in times of sadness, so too they may be drawn from Spirit to be supportive once again.

I recall crying myself to sleep one night, and suddenly I felt a change in the vibrations in the room and I sat upright in bed. There I saw my deceased beagle Bonnie float through the closed French doors that lead from the bedroom to the veranda and jump on the end of my bed. Although I couldn't see her solid form on the bed, there was an indent in the bedcovers, and when I leant to touch the bed, it was warm. It was so comforting to know my dear friend had come to reassure me that I was not alone in my struggle.

My son was devastated when his dog Rocky was run over, only to have a double blow when the priest at his school told him animals do not go to heaven. I am here to tell you there is infinite proof from my own family's experience and that of clients—and what I have witnessed as a psychic medium—that there is definitely a transition from an earthly plane to the afterlife for your pets.

39

Saying goodbye to beloved pets

I care not for a man's religion whose dog and cat are
not the better for it.
Abraham Lincoln

Beloved pets are part of our family, they're our mates, our companions and our children. They are our lives. Thereby it is very fitting they should be given as much consideration to having an 'end-of-life' ritual. A pet's love is unconditional and they intuitively know that their owners are doing the best they can for their ultimate wellbeing. You may like to hold their paw, stroke their fur, speaking soothing words of comfort and love; even if their eyes are closed they will sense your energies and feel your devotion.

I'm lucky my parents' home has a very large backyard. The next-door neighbour has some wonderful tropical palm trees that graciously fan over the adjoining fence, providing a little refuge in the corner. Over the years, this special place has become our pet cemetery. Pet birds, mice, goldfish, dogs and cats have all been laid to rest there; and when my children have lost their pets, they too have joined my childhood memories in this little haven. It's a place that has brought comfort for the family to know our pets are close by.

Some pets we chose to bury with their food bowl, special blanket or toys. If you have a child's pet that has passed over, encourage your child to consider some things they may wish to include in the burial of their pet. Let them have some thought in what they think their pet would like to take on its journey to the afterlife. After all, the Egyptians were great believers in farewelling their dead with an assortment of aids to assist their transition from one world to the next.

A little prayer or a favourite song can be recited as part of their fond farewell. Ritual and ceremony can be a wonderful asset in the farewell and grief process. You may encourage them to draw or write a story about the cute things the pet did or fun times they had together on holidays. Children can grieve differently, for some anger may be the way they express their emotions. So it's important their teacher be notified of a death of a special pet or someone close to monitor them should there be changes in their behaviour so a sympathetic approach can be had.

Although you might wish to shelter your child from the pain of the death of a pet, it's a wonderful educational tool and experience to understand the process of the stages of life. You are aiding and assisting your child to understand the concepts of this world and the afterlife.

The adjustment to the loss of your special mate, friend and family member will take time; after all they gave you so much affection and unconditional love. Their quirky little personalities lit up your life when you walked in from a hard day at work. The daily routine you or your children had of feeding, giving them water, grooming, taking them for a walk in the park or rolling with them in the backyard will be now be absent. Their companionship will be missed. They were an extension of your life. Many pets will try and keep these bonds of affection close, just as Sue found out with BJ.

The grey mist

Sue and I became friends when I was looking for a new dog for the children after Rocky passed. Money was indeed tight back in those days and Brendan had seen the film *The Adventures of Milo and Otis* and had firmly made up his mind he wanted a male pug dog—like the one in the movie. Scanning the Saturday paper for advertisements for pugs, all seemed financially way out of our reach. They were in vogue due to the high celebrity status they had achieved in the movie—every child wanted a pug. I had to tell Brendan there was no way I could give him his heart's desire.

'But you said I could pick the next dog—it's not fair,' he said.

What could I do? Well, as I have always been taught when I was growing up—hand the problem over to Spirit. So I sat on the veranda and said a silent prayer to the universe—'Help me!' I had an overwhelming feeling to go back to the newspaper and read the ads again. As though it were highlighted in my imagination, one particular ad stood out. I had a feeling that the owner had a problem and I had the solution. So I rang. Yes, she did have puppies, but the price was out of my range. But the seller, Sue, suggested that before purchasing a pug we should come and visit, as they can snort and make funny noises that some people can never adjust to.

Later I found out that she was very particular about who took her dogs. Sue lived in Bargo, which was a good two hours drive from where we lived at Castle Hill, and the cost of petrol would be an issue on the tight weekly budget we lived on. I couldn't spare the cash for fuel, let along the dog. Within an hour of handing the matter over to Spirit, however, the unexpected happened. I received a phone call from an agitated person wanting an urgent reading. The donation from the reading enabled us to fill up the car, have a meal on the road and see the puppies.

I rang Sue back and said we were coming, and later she said how strange she thought it was for us to be coming out to look at puppies in the dark! She'd just put all the pups to bed for the night in the garage, but there was no stopping us as we made the lengthy trip out into the bush on the outskirts of Sydney. Brendan enjoyed playing with the pups and grown-up dogs in the garage while Sue and I had a cup of coffee. As we talked, we discovered we had so much in common in spiritual beliefs. And in turn, I was able to share my gift and give her the answer she needed at that time.

We thought it amazing that her prized black pug BJ had the same nickname as my youngest son, Brendan Joseph. It was just the confirmation she needed—that we were ideal potential owners for one of her pugs. She was more than happy for us to have one of the puppies when we could afford it.

Then she said, 'Georgina, I know you're after a pup, but one of my first breeding female pugs, Candy, needs a good home with much love and affection. Would you consider taking her instead of a pup? This would be a gift—no charge. I just need her to go to a home where I know she'll be loved.' Tears welled up in my eyes just as Brendan walked in from playing with Danny, a one-year-old pug. The two had hit it off immediately, developing an instant rapport, running backwards and forwards in the garage.

'What's up, Mum? Why are you crying?'

When I told him the exciting news, he said, 'That's nice.'

Sue sensed there was an issue, and asked him, 'What's up, mate? What's the problem?'

'Well, I love Danny. He's the dog I want.'

I could have fallen over backwards with embarrassment. There was silence for a moment, and then Sue turned to me and said, 'You can have both dogs, on one condition, that when I need Danny for breeding he's available.'

That evening we became proud owners of not one but two pugs, at no cost. It certainly is an amazing story of two women meeting each other's needs. It is a connection that's lasted more than thirteen years now. Sue's love for her pugs has extended beyond the grave, and she recently recounted BJ's life to me:

BJ was my first black pug. It was love at first sight when I bought him. He wasn't the pick of the litter, but he was mine. It was a soul connection—we just clicked. He was so close to me, and I him. When I had all my lengthy surgeries, he would sleep on my bed all the time. He was my little comforter, my little man. BJ seemed to know if I was down and would always snuggle up to me. He was eleven years old when he passed. He had lost the use of his back legs and had arthritis. He had to be put to sleep because his body was failing him. So I had him cremated and brought him home where he sits on the mantelpiece.

After his passing, I always felt that he was still around me. The first time I saw something was when his breeder came to stay and we were going to a show with our young pugs. It was probably a couple of months after he'd passed. We were in the kitchen and I saw a flash of something go across the room. It happened to me a couple of times, and we both said, 'BJ's here for a visit'. It was a quick-moving grey shadow. Sometimes when I'm on my own and have young dogs that I'm attending to, I feel his presence, and at times I've noticed the dogs will seem to be looking and reacting to something unseen. A couple of times when I've had pups born from his line, black pugs, I see a grey mist and feel his presence. It gives me great comfort and happiness to know he's around.

Just like in our household, we had suffered a loss and were looking for a replacement, you may well undergo a similar situation where children are involved. A possible suggestion would be that the family research what kind of pet would suit your family's personality and needs. Will it be long-hair or short-hair, big stature or minute? And how about temperament—do we want a lazy dog who'll sit by our feet, or do we want an active dog we'll have to walk each day?

You can encourage talk about the special qualities your previous pet had and the not-so-pleasant aspects of their personality, such as barking for hours when you left for shopping. You may wish to use the example of how science has proven the beneficial effects an animal has on a human, selecting specific breeds of dogs who can be trained to be the eyes of someone blind, the ears for the deaf, and tune in to vibrational change in brain activity for their master who is epileptic and sense a seizure is coming on. Pets are now being taken into nursing and aged care facilities as their contribution as a great therapeutic aid to the elderly and infirmed is now acknowledged. They are selected for their nature and placidity. After all, their role is of a special kind of counsellor or therapist. I know some families who have chosen to rescue a pet from an animal shelter, giving them a second chance at life!

When I was considering purchasing a cat, I had a vivid dream there was a tortoiseshell at the local Cat Protection Society. The next morning I rang to make enquiries, and if they have such a cat—in fact they had two. I hurried down and it was obvious which cat I was going to choose—her paw kept poking out of the cage to grab my attention. Had her soul sent me a telepathic message she was available for adoption? I called her Miracle, for it was a miracle she'd been given a second chance. Well, if there's wisdom in the saying 'cats have nine lives', Miracle is on her second—or perhaps she's already been full circle and reincarnated a number of times!

40

Moving forward

There comes a special moment in everyone's life, a
moment for which that person was born. That special
opportunity, when he seizes it, will fulfil his mission—a
mission for which he is uniquely qualified. In that
moment, he finds greatness. It is his finest hour.

Winston Churchill

D o not be afraid that death is final. You have lived this life
before and will almost certainly return again through reincarnation to continue the lessons and choices you have
made with your soul's grouping on this earth. There are no final
goodbyes, as there is no death, only an intermission between
heaven and earth while you are waiting to be reborn to experience another karmic path.

So what do you do and accomplish 'in the meantime' until we
meet again in another lifetime? There exists now a powerful opportunity for your soul's development and happiness to look at special

ways to celebrate and remember the special soul connection that existed with your dearly departed.

Reclaiming life

Grace had watched her husband, Richard, slip away with leukemia. It had been five long months, eventually ending with a vigil by his bedside. Samantha, their five-year-old daughter, would clamber up on her daddy's bed and rest her little dark curly head upon his chest. She felt reassured when she could feel the beat of his heart. A year had slipped by since his death, and now Grace was seeking some direction in her life with a General/Futuristic reading.

It was most evident that this vibrant 33-year-old was exhausted. She had turned her grief inward, focusing on Samantha's needs, trying to be both mother and father. She admitted that she felt cheated, and had been building up some frustration and resentment now that she was left alone to raise her little one. Would she have another relationship, someone who would love her and her daughter? They were a package deal after all. She needed to reclaim her life.

Grace needed to focus on the basics—to get back to healthy, nutritious foods, and to have take-away food only as a 'treat' instead of every meal. Her physical life had been stagnant and she didn't see where she could fit in an exercise routine with Samantha's daily activities. Looking at her options, I thought hiring an exercise bike would allow her to oversee her child's activities while using pedal power.

Weekends could include a fun walk by the beach or in a park. And by buying a kite for Samantha and herself, it would be like waving to Daddy up in the sky. They may even choose to place a little kiss on the wings of the kite and see how far the wind could take their loving kisses to the heavens. It would be a fun activity that included exercise, and they would have some happy moments in nature playing together.

I could see that the power of touch through massage would be of great benefit to Grace, and a practitioner who could work with the subtle energies of the auric field and clear built-up nega-tivity would definitely give Grace a feeling of release. I'm so fortunate to know one such person who possesses all these skills, plus she is a master of psychotherapy—Alison. The timing was just right for Grace to start her inward journey to release her pain and look at formulating some direction for her future. I knew she and Alison would be the right match.

Next it was time to look at something new—a skill or a hobby that she had always wanted to do, but never got around to. Instantly, Spirit showed me a pair of bright red dancing shoes. Had she considered dancing? Grace laughed. Just before she met Richard she was enquiring about enrolling in Latin-American classes. Bingo! Thanks Spirit, you knew exactly what she needed.

Grace felt guilty about leaving Samantha with a caregiver. Money was not the issue; it was the security of knowing they only had each other. There was the need to wean each other from this codependence. Two hours would be the first little break while she met up with a girlfriend for coffee; then perhaps the next break would be half a day. It would be a slow but steady adjustment for all.

Grace could implement these small steps immediately, and I felt Alison would take her on her journey of her self-discovery.

Tears welled up in her eyes—she still felt heavy-hearted on special days such as Father's Day and Valentine's Day. How could she overcome the grief for both of them? She had purchased a beautiful carved camphor box for Samantha to place special paintings and craftwork she did at school for her daddy to 'see' which sat at the end of her bed. But she needed a practical ritual beyond the house that would see both of them getting excited. I suggested she consider naming a star after her husband. On special days, such as his birthday, both she and Samantha could go to a local observatory and look at 'Daddy' shining down and smiling on them from his heavenly home. A huge grin appeared on her face—she could do this.

I then suggested that when Samantha had a birthday or a special painting or message she wanted to give to Daddy, that they purchase some helium balloons and tie a very small piece of cake, or the painting, to the balloon and send it to heaven, just for Daddy.

'Samantha loves balloons, why didn't I ever think of that?' Grace said. 'I've searched high and low for grief books for children, but none with practical rituals. Can you guess what Sam and I will be doing this weekend?'

Grace bounded out of my apartment, a woman on a mission. Richard's life was to be a celebration.

Dealing with the hurt of loss

Individuals and families can differ in the ways they experience grief, much like the waves of the ocean coming up and down. So too some individuals will appear to be riding the crest of their grief— they seem controlled and functioning well in society, but they may suddenly become aware of their beloved's favourite perfume or hear their favourite song and come undone. A special day such as Christmas, a birthday or anniversary can trigger a sudden temporary surge of grief and they appear to come down with a crash.

Know that this is normal—grief is a process and not an event. Seeking professional help from a well-trained counsellor, general practitioner, priest or minister, or attending a grief support group, will allow those who are suffering to feel supported in the loving presence of others. It can provide a place where they feel they can talk about their loved one, receive encouragement and learn 'tools' for strategies to deal with their loss.

Different styles of grieving

It is thought that there are two styles of grieving, with the majority of people using a combination of both. When using the 'intuitive approach', individuals seek out social support and tend to focus on their emotional aspects of loss, around managing their feelings. For others, they will adapt the 'instrumental approach', focusing on thinking about their loss; their grief is often expressed through activity and problem solving.

Grace unknowingly used a combination of both of these styles of grieving to assist her and Samantha in dealing with Richard's passing. Grace was all Samantha had, and Samantha looked to her mum to learn how to understand her dad's death. Grace was honest, open, and gave her clear and direct information about her dad's condition. Samantha was allowed to participate in his funeral—she placed her favourite teddy bear in his coffin when they viewed the body because she felt he needed something to cuddle up to when the nights got cold.

Grace had thought long and hard about how she would get Samantha through Richard's passing. Perhaps if Samantha had been a teenager, it would have been a different story—teenage ways of coping sometimes create tension with other adults. Staying out late with friends, playing loud music and not showering are typical types of adolescent behaviour dealing with the normal issues of independence and separation from parents. Yet these developmental tasks can interfere with their capacity to receive support from the adults around them in dealing with their grief.

Well, thankfully for Grace, Samantha was only five years old. However, after a year of struggling and trying to be both mother and father to Samantha, Grace's health was starting to fail her. The medical professions do acknowledge that grief can cause a reduction in the functioning of the immune system, leading to colds, influenza, anxiety, sleeping difficulties and depression.

Luckily for Grace, she could see where she was heading and she sought help. If you feel this way, or someone close to you points out that you seem to be suffering from some of these symptoms, seek the help of a professional immediately—after all, your dearly departed would only want the very best for you in health and vitality.

41

Life is a celebration

Be faithful in small things because it is in them
that your strength lies.
Mother Teresa

Where do you begin? How do you cope with the memory
of someone you loved so much, who was so dear to
you, whose life and love was so treasured? Sometimes
actions speak louder than words, and being in a state of 'doing'
can assist you in the processes of taking baby steps forward towards
tomorrow. So I have compiled a list of inspirational (remember
inspiration means 'in-Spirit') ways to honour your dearly departed.

Honour your loved one

There are many ways to cherish the memory of your loved ones
after they have crossed over so that their memory lives on. You
could start a daily journal or diary, writing down your feelings, happy
moments together, holidays enjoyed, little sayings that you shared.

Learn to verbally express your feelings to others, the good and the not so good. Remember, a problem shared is a problem halved.

Consider having a dedicated space for your dearly departed. This could be a table, mantelpiece or a shrine with precious photos, memorabilia, perfume, hairbrush, jewellery and toys; something that gives your senses an instant recall of your loved one. You could also compile a photo album, scrapbook or slide show of their life to share with relatives and friends. Remembering the good times keeps your heart warm with fond thoughts and times shared.

To honour your loved one in the local community, donate a book prize to a local school or educational institute in your beloved's name; consider a perpetual scholarship for a disadvantaged person or student named in their honour; or plant a tree to sustain the environment for future generations. Another idea could be to start a charity in their name to assist others who have similar interests or disadvantages. If they were a returned serviceperson, have someone march in their place on memorial days. Be proud of their achievements and what they stood for.

On anniversaries, birthdays and sacred days, relive your loved one's life by reminding yourself of five things that would have brought them joy on that occasion. If they rang a special friend, keep the tradition alive; if they bought a present for a homeless person, do the same. It is the little things we remember and do that spark a light within our soul as we bring to mind how precious they were.

If your child has lost one of their parents, a grandparent or an animal, you may consider purchasing a special box, to be placed in the child's bedroom, there to be used to store and collect letters, postcards, paintings, birthday cards and celebration items they would have loved to share. They can write stories about their special pet and the good times they enjoyed together. You may even like to put the beloved's name on the box, just as Samantha did in loving memory of her dad.

Little treasures become storehouses of instant memories, soft ways of actively participating while grieving for those who have passed on. Maybe they would like to bury the pet's toy with their pet. Children grieve in different ways to adults, and allowing them a special tool to work through grief is healthy. Don't forget to notify their school teacher about any death in the family—this will allow them to better understand that the child has a change in their behaviour. With each action, there becomes an active way of holding the essences of love and devotion alive in the minds and hearts of those who are loved.

As Jess sat down for her reading, I couldn't help but notice the suffering in her eyes and how frail she looked. Her hands shook as she pulled out a picture of her boyfriend, Benjamin, the reason for her a 'Dearly Departed' session. As I tuned in, I could hear ambulance sirens and I saw police at the base of a tall building. My eyes were then drawn to a balcony—I sensed there had been a fall. I heard a man's voice with a thick South African accent—it was Benjamin coming through. He stood behind Jess, placing both his hands on her shoulders as if to still her presence.

'Tell her I'm proud of the decision she's made for my ashes. I know the pain and suffering this has brought. I'm at peace with her choice—it's right for half to go home to my parents and the remainder to be scattered here. I considered both countries my home,' Benjamin told me.

Jess had tears flowing down her face, but her colour had now returned.

'Does that make sense, Jess?' I asked. She went on to explain that she met Benjamin while travelling in South Africa. When she returned to Australia six months later, he followed. He fell in love with her and the country. They were partying at a friend's apartment when Benjamin stepped out for a cigarette, lost his balance and fell many floors to his death.

She had to organise the funeral and cremation by herself, and then make the decision regarding his ashes. She wanted to keep him close by, but since he was an only child, she knew his parents also expressed the same sentiments. The reading had now given her confirmation; her decision had been correct. Benjamin's ashes had been cremated and divided into two urns; one was to return to South Africa, where his parents were to scatter his ashes on his favourite beach, and Jess had thought she would take the other half of the ashes to the mountains where the couple spent so much of their free time.

'Georgina, I know he would love to rest overlooking the valley where we spent many weekends,' she said.

You too may wish to consider a special place filled with memories or significance for you and your beloved. Several of my clients have chosen to place some of their special person's ashes in a locket they wear around their neck. You could also plant a bush or tree at the cemetery, plot or crematorium, and tend to it with love and attention. One of my clients had her beloved dog preserved, like in the museums, and her companion sits in her lounge room watching over her daily life.

To help children through their process of grief, encourage them to attach a small piece of birthday cake, a painting or a card to a helium balloon (you may need more than one balloon), to be allowed to fly up into the sky, giving the child the concept of heaven and earth. Or they could adopt the kite-flying exercise, like Samantha did. Another nice way to keep the memory alive is to name a star after their dearly departed. On anniversaries or birthdays, visit the local observatory to view your special person shining down upon you. If your child is frightened of the dark, this can be a very special way of letting them know they are being watched and protected, with the rays of light beaming down on them as they sleep.

Complete a project your loved one had started, for example finishing the gardening, or raising money for the local building fund; and if your loved one had a planned holiday to a special destination, consider fulfilling that dream in their honour.

If you're getting married, carry a small picture of your dearly departed in your bouquet or in your suit pocket, as though they're walking down the aisle with you on that special day. A photo of your loved one can be placed in the floral decorations on the bridal table, facing the bride and groom, giving them a special place and honouring their contribution to the family and keeping their memory alive.

It was approaching the first anniversary of Victoria's passing. Ralph had been a devoted husband and was finally opening his heart to love again. He had been dating a new woman for almost two months, and he felt within his spirit that he needed to do something in Victoria's memory but he didn't know what. He could see a new life unfolding for his future and was torn in which direction to go.

I suggested he consider a ritual, as I have discovered with other clients that adopting some aspect of a ritual can be very helpful in the grief process. I asked him to consider a 'farewell ceremony'.

Victoria and Ralph had loved fishing at the lakes, so I suggested he make a paper boat and write 'Victoria' on the side. Was there something he wanted to tell her, perhaps 'Thank you' or 'I love you'? Maybe he could write this inside the boat, or just say it to himself as he placed the boat on the waters at the high tide, allowing the receding waters to take it on a final journey of setting their connection free.

Another ritual can be to light a candle in your loved one's honour, either weekly or on special occasions, to bring a wonderful sense of reverence and calm into your life.

Don't go to pieces—honour their life by cherishing your own. Eat healthily, have regular medical check-ups, get plenty of sleep, learn to laugh again and rent plenty of comedy DVDs. Laughter is great medicine for the soul. Become active—try gardening, visiting the gym, walking and spending time in nature to recharge your batteries. Bathing yourself in spiritual awareness can aid grieving by allowing a better understanding of the life and death process. Investigate spirituality, religion and different philosophies.

To move on with your life, make a start with a new hobby or craft, or join a different social group. If you're active and happy, your dearly departed will feel more freedom. Keep spiritual stillness by learning to meditate or taking an active meditation course in tai chi or qigong.

Volunteer work can also help overcome grief; when you're helping others, you have less time to be self-absorbed and depressed. Keep a gratitude diary to remind yourself of the good things in life. Each day, write down five things to appreciate. They can be as simple as being grateful for the fresh air you breathe, the food you have in your fridge, the friend who rang you today, a comfortable bed to sleep in and a safe haven to rest after the day's activities.

Many people continue to grieve in subtle ways, one step at a time, and one day at a time. Consider embracing a form of ritual, be it daily, weekly or yearly. This can assist in the process of moving forward, while still honouring your loved one's memory to burn bright within your hearts and minds.

Life doesn't end, love goes on. We are always loved, helped and watched over by our dearly departeds.

I would like to leave you with the following story to ponder and reflect on as you move towards tomorrow on your own soul's journey.

Two wolves—A traditional Native American story

One evening an old Cherokee told his grandson about a battle that goes on inside people.

He said: 'My son, the battle is between two "wolves" inside us all. One is Evil. It is anger, envy, jealousy, sorrow, regret, greed, arrogance, self-pity, guilt, resentment, inferiority, lies, false pride, superiority and ego. The other is Good. It is joy, peace, love, hope, serenity, humility, kindness, benevolence, empathy, generosity, truth, compassion and faith.'

The grandson thought about it for a minute and then asked his grandfather, 'Which wolf wins?'

The old Cherokee simply replied, 'The one you feed.'

Resources

Books

Chopra, Deepak, *Life after Death*, Harmony Books, London, 2006
Hardo, Trutz, *Children Who Have Lived Before*, Rider, London, 2005
Knight, Sirona, *The Book of Reincarnation*, Barrons, New York, 2002
Kuhl, MD, David, *What Dying People Want*, ABC Books, Sydney, 2005
Miller, PhD, Sukie, *After Death*, Touchstone, New York, 1998
Van Praagh, James, *Heaven and Earth*, Simon & Schuster, New York, 2001
Van Praagh, James, *Healing Grief*, Hodder, Sydney, 2000
Van Praagh, James, *Talking to Heaven*, Hodder, Sydney, 1998
Various, *The Essential Dictionary of Quotations*, Hinkler Books, Dingley, 1992
Weiss, Brian, *Same Soul, Many Bodies*, Piatkus Books, London, 2004
Weiss, Brian, *Many Lives, Many Masters*, Simon & Schuster, New York, 1988
Williamson, Linda, *Children and the Spirit World*, Piatkus Books, London, 1997

Websites

About.com, *Death & Dying*, dying.about.com [27 June 2007, 25 August 2007]
Anncath-Roby, Catherine and Byron Pulsifer, *Inspirational Words of Wisdom*, www.wow4u.com/death-dying-quotes/index.html [26 August 2007]
Australian National University, *Australian Dictionary of Biography—Online Edition*, www.adb.online.anu.edu.au/biogs/A110409b.htm [19 May 2007]

Centre for Leadership for Women, *Memorable Quotes*,
   www.leadershipforwomen.com.au/quotes.htm [4 September 2007]
Enough is Enough Anti-Violence Movement Inc, *An Interview with Ken
   Marslew*, www.enoughisenough.org.au/interview [5 June 2007]
Enough is Enough Anti-Violence Movement Inc, *The Peacemaker PDF*,
   www.enoughisenough.org.au/assets/file/pd/the_peacemaker/pdf [5 June
   2007]
Faze Magazine Canada, Eileen Harrigan, *The Dalai Lama*,
   www.fazeteen.com/winter2001/dalailama.htm [19 June 2007]
HeartMath LLC, *HeartQuotes: Quotes of the Heart*,
   heartquotes.net/communication.html [26 August 2007]
Hollow Hill, Fiona Broome, Eibhlin Morey MacIntosh, *Historical
   Quotations about Ghosts and Hauntings*, www.hollowhill.com/historic-
   quotes.htm [25 August 2007]
In the Light of Angels, *Angel and Inspirational Quotes*,
   www.angelslight.org/quotes.html [26 August 2007]
Journey of Hearts, Kirsti A. Dyer MD, *United in Courage and Grief*,
   www.journeyofhearts.org/kirstimd/911_quote.htm [19 August 2007]
Michael Moncur, The Quotations Page, *Quotations by Subject: Inspiration*,
   www.quotationspage.com/subjects/inspiration [19 June 2007]
Native American, traditional, *The White Buffalo*, Mercer Online,
   www.merceronline.com/Native/native05.htm [13 May 2007]
Notable Quotes, *Quotes on the Soul*, www.notable-
   quotes.com/s/soul_quotes.html [24 June 2007]
RIGPA, *The Tibetan Book of Living and Dying*,
   rigpa.org/helping_the_dying.html [27 August 2007]
Sacred Dying Foundation, *The Vigil Programs*, www.sacreddying.org/vigil-
   programs.htm [29 April 2007]
Sam Meilach, *Other Spiritual Quotes*,
   www.meilach.com/spiritual/misc/other.html [24 June 2007]
Soul Future Spiritual and Dream Interpretation Site, Carine Rudman,
   Inspirational Quotes on the Mind,
   www.soulfuture.com/inspirational_quotes/iq_mind.asp [31 August
   2007]

Various, *Caduceus*, Wikipedia, en.wikipedia.org/wiki/Caduceus [15 May 2007]

Victorian Government, *Better Health Channel*, www.betterhealth.vic.gov.au [25 January 2007]

Wisdom Quotes: Quotations to Inspire and Challenge, Jone Johnson Lewis, *Gratitude Quotes*, www.wisdomquotes.com/cat_gratitude.html [25 August 2007]

Wisdom Quotes: Quotations to Inspire and Challenge, Jone Johnson Lewis, *Heaven Quotes*, www.wisdomquotes.com/cat_heaven.html [31 August 2007]

Zaadz Community, *Quotes about Death*, www.zaadz.com/quotes/topics/death [27 June 2007]

Zaadz Community, *Quotes about Hell*, www.zaadz.com/quotes/topics/hell [27 August 2007]

Zaadz Community, *Quotes about Intuition*, www.zaadz.com/quotes/topics/intuition [25 August 2007]

Zaadz Community, *Quotes about Pain*, www.zaadz.com/quotes/topics/pain [27 August 2007]

Zaadz Community, *Quotes about Prayer*, www.zaadz.com/quotes/topics/prayer [29 August 2007]

Zaadz Community, *Quotes about Soul*, www.zaadz.com/quotes/topics/soul [24 June 2007]

Zaadz Community, *Quotes about Suicide*, www.zaadz.com/quotes/topics/suicide [26 June 2007]

Everyday Encounters with Those Who have Passed Over, and What They Teach about Life After Death

This heart-warming book details numerous experiences people have had with loved ones who have died; from funny incidents and amazing synchronicities to guidance by departed loved ones. What makes this new book extra special is that each story contains an insight, which explains a little more about the spirit world, showing how those who have passed on continue to take an interest in our lives.

These accounts show how there are always unexpected moments of magic to be found in amongst the grief of the loss of those we love.

Georgina travels the world as a guest lecturer, teacher, reader, and hosts Sacred Journeys. To learn more about her work and schedule, you may find information on her website:

www.georginawalker.com

inspired
LIVING

Welcome to Inspired Living—soulful books for mind, body and spirit...

Inspired Living books cover a range of areas including wellness, psychology, spirituality, ancient wisdom and divination. All our authors have something special to offer. Chosen with everyday concerns in mind, their books will enrich your life in a practical yet meaningful way.

To find out more about our books or to join our monthly e-newsletter see www.inspiredliving.net.au